Some Trust In Chariots

Looking Through the Glass Darkly Series

Jim & Vicki Gordon

Copyright © 2015 T Ministries.

All rights reserved solely by the author. The author guarantees all contents are original and do not infringe upon the legal rights of any other person or work. No part of this book may be reproduced in any form without the permission of the author.

All scripture used is from the King James Version and was taken from Sword Searcher version 7 software.

ISBN#978-1-61119-140-0

Printed in the United States of America.

Printed by Calvary Publishing

A Ministry of Parker Memorial Baptist Church

1902 East Cavannaugh Road

Lansing, Michigan 48910

www.CalvaryPublishing.org

I am crucified with Christ: nevertheless I live; yet not I, but Christ liveth in me: and the life which I now live in the flesh I live by the faith of the Son of God, who loved me, and gave himself for me. (Galatians 2:20 KJV)

Visit our ministry web site at:

www.tclministries.org

The Crucified Life Ministries

Sign up for our daily devotion

We are excited for the opportunity God has given our ministry **The Crucified Life Ministries,** a ministry of our local Baptist Church, to write a second devotional book **The Looking Through the Glass Darkly Devotional Series.**

We pray as you read this book **Some Trust in Chariots**, in addition to your personal daily Bible reading and studying, that God richly blesses your desire to know more about Him and His Word.

God calls us to sojourn upon this earth; not to dwell placing roots into anything of this world. As His spiritual family God desires we choose to live as strangers or peculiar persons upon this earth as His Holy Spirit dwells within us directing and leading our steps unto things of God.

Our eternal citizenship is based upon God's great mercy, grace, and love as we rest upon His finished work on the cross at Calvary. He alone provided payment in full for all sin; past, present, and future having nothing to do with any works of mankind. Our eternal spiritual outlook rests upon a future with God forever through the great and lasting promises of His living Word.

The Bible tells us since sin entered into the world all mankind have been born with a sentence of death:

For the wages of sin is death; but the gift of God is eternal life through Jesus Christ our Lord. (Romans 6:23 KJV)

And as it is appointed unto men once to die, but after this the judgment: (Hebrews 9:27 KJV)

A time to be born, and a time to die; a time to plant, and a time to pluck up that which is planted; (Ecclesiastes 3:2 KJV)

If we stop right here with only a biblical understanding one day we all must physically die because of the wages of sin why would mankind have hope for the future? If all we had to look forward to was an eventual physical death and the death of our family and friends, or an end to life instead of a beginning; why would anyone desire to look with an eternally established anticipation and earnest towards the future?

But God did not stop in death but overcame death bringing about the possibility of eternal life for whosoever shall believe:

O death, where is thy sting? O grave, where is thy victory? The sting of death is sin; and the strength of sin is the law. But thanks be to God, which giveth us the victory through our Lord Jesus Christ. Therefore, my beloved brethren, be ye stedfast, unmoveable, always abounding in the work of the Lord, forasmuch as ye know that your labour is not in vain in the Lord. (1 Corinthians 15:55-58 KJV)

All praise goes to God for He did not leave life hanging in the balance with an ending of certain physical death. God took the sting out of physical death giving all mankind the opportunity to spiritually live eternally with Him forever.

Does the thought of your own personal physical death upon this earth cause you to become anxious bringing questions to your mind about your own spiritual journey upon the narrow pathway from earth into the heavenly realm? A deeper look into the object you have placed your trust and security in is of great importance to the place of your eternal future home.

The Bible clearly tells us in 1st John 5:13:

These things have I written unto you that believe on the name of the Son of God; that ye may know that ye have eternal life, and that ye may believe on the name of the Son of God. (1 John 5:13 KJV)

The Bible clearly says that we can be sure of having an eternal resting place after our physical death upon this earth instead of agony in the fires of Hell for all eternity.

If you do not have a personal relationship with God through trust placed in His Son Jesus Christ. Or you have doubts or questions circling through your mind and heart concerning where you will personally spend eternity; whether it will be in the fires of Hell or in Heaven with God we encourage you to read the Bible because faith and trust in Him come from the supernatural power of His Word:

For whosoever shall call upon the name of the Lord shall be saved. How then shall they call on him in whom they have not believed? and how shall they believe in him of whom they have not heard? and how shall they hear without a preacher? And how shall they preach, except they be sent? as it is written, How beautiful are the feet of them that preach the gospel of peace, and bring glad tidings of good things! (Romans 10:13-15 KJV)

So then faith cometh by hearing, and hearing by the word of God. (Romans 10:17 KJV)

Please seek out a pastor or close Christian friend who can talk and pray with you personally regarding your eternal future who can show you how you can know for sure you are on the narrow pathway leading to an eternal life and peace with God forever in Heaven.

Life and death for all mankind is in the hands of an eternal God who loves all mankind, including you!

I am he that liveth, and was dead; and, behold, I am alive for evermore, Amen; and have the keys of hell and of death. (Revelation 1:18 KJV)

Let Him be the Author and Finisher of your life.

We would like to take this opportunity to give much thanks to our local church family and pastor who provides spiritual teaching and leadership planted firmly in the Word of God encouraging our spiritual growth and living unto God as we sojourn upon this earth.

Some devotions included in this book also appear on our web site at www.tclministries.org and may appear in a different format or with changes made to wording, but within margins of the context of scripture, in final editing for this book.

Other books written by the author include:

Looking Through the Glass Darkly

Table of Contents

Some Trust in Chariots 13

A Biblical History of Chariots 15

Acts of Wavering Faith.. 19

Behold There Came A Leper 22

A Hard Right Turn 25

A Peculiar People 26

All about Hell 29

Until the Robe Adorns You 31

The Test of Fire 32

A City without Walls 35

A Humble and Useful Vessel Mete for Christ 37

My Yoke is Easy.. 39

Seek Not To Be Loosed 42

Hath God Said..46

Spiritual Adoption.. 51

The Three Triune God 56

Holy Living... 62

Sealed by the Holy Spirit... 68

Righteous Judgment According to God's Word 69

Loose Him and Let Him Go 74

Loving AND Judging Others 75

A Financial Song and Dance 78

Who Is Responsible for Jesus's Death? 88

Are You Living to Die?	92
Is there life after death?	95
Is Heaven a real place?	98
Spiritual Dry Bones	99
Is Your Manna Moldy?	104
What's the Difference?	109
Noah's Ark	113
Salvation is Simple	119
In God's Waiting Room	124
Payment OF Sin	127
The Pride of the King	130
Pattern for Prayer	132
Can Woman Preach?	136
Death of a Pet	138
A Prayerless Nation	141
The Truth Slices Like A Knife	143
Piloting a Hot Air Balloon	144
A Rainbow of Promise	148
Hidden Manna and a white Stone	151
Hell is a Real Place	156
What Garment Adorns You?	160
Calling the Church	162
A Helpmeet For Man	164
Guarded On All Sides	168

Hagar Ran Away	172
But God Moments	175
Hurdles Can Be Self-Inflicted Barriers	177
Paul Was Willing to Suffer	181
The Twenty Four Hour Media Circus	183
Self-Sacrifice in Serving Him	186
Bringing Every Thought Into Captivity	191
Remember Lot's Wife?	194
Flesh of Ishmael, The Promise of Isaac	196

Some Trust in Chariots

Some trust in chariots, and some in horses: but we will remember the name of the LORD our God. They are brought down and fallen: but we are risen, and stand upright. Save, LORD: let the king hear us when we call. (Psalms 20:7-9 KJV)

David concludes this psalm by proclaiming He and his people place their trust in the Lord God, not in themselves, things, or in their military strength, which in those times included many horses and chariots marching into battle.

Woe to them that go down to Egypt for help; and stay on horses, and trust in chariots, because they are many; and in horsemen, because they are very strong; but they look not unto the Holy One of Israel, neither seek the LORD! (Isaiah 31:1KJV)

Sometimes it is easier to put your trust in what you can clearly see with your eyes those things existing right before you, as men see, not giving a thought to placing trust in the words of The Lord without having visual and tangible confirmation directly in front of you.

Sometimes the Lord asks us to crawl out unto the end of the limb, or at the edge of a cliff, or climb that high looming mountain or as we wait patiently for His divine direction and timing before taking our next step. He does promise to be our personal battle warrior in all our bouts, if we allow Him to lead us, in His perfect timing, through any situation at hand according to His will and way; not our way!

The very same battles as were fought in biblical times still abound today. We no longer use horses and chariots to rush into physical battle with opponents but many still place faith and hope in all military branches of government and the mighty military strength and power; especially in America.

These same citizens often rely upon "modern day chariots" including handouts of governmental subsidies and other public funds, human abilities, and military endeavors, and highly technological advances for protection of life and liberty and for their ultimate physical and spiritual victory. This faulty thinking pattern does not leave room for an all-powerful or omnipotent God who is always able and ready to fight all our battles; whatever the source of the conflict or situation may be.

All battles, whether they are: spiritual or physical enemies, God can swiftly lead us through to victory on the other side as we keep our eyes focused upon Him and not the circumstances surrounding us.

FOR FURTHER CONTEMPLATION:

When we trust in God He keeps us upright against *all* enemies; whether they be spiritual or physical.

A Biblical History of Chariots

When thou goest out to battle against thine enemies, and seest horses, and chariots, and a people more than thou, be not afraid of them: for the LORD thy God is with thee, which brought thee up out of the land of Egypt. (Deuteronomy 20:1KJV)

Ancient chariots for clashes were actually portable battle stations loaded with everything necessary: including persons, ammunition, and multiple weaponry. The chariots were small but quick and nimble and could be readily maneuvered around in times of war near the front lines of the battle. Chariots were likely pulled along by working animals such as horses, donkeys, or mules.

Chariots had a platform for standing upon and commonly laying upon either two or four wheels. There was a lot of variance in the size, weight, and ease of maneuverability of chariots throughout the ancient biblical world. Often, when turning on a quick note chariots could easily flip over in the heat of the battle.

There were a wide variety of designs used throughout ancient societies. It was tough, but not impossible, for those more highly gifted in knowledge and technology of their day, to design a vehicle that could provide stability and ease as well as be nimble for an edge in combat situations.

Yes, technology in biblical times was moving forward and advancing. (And you thought mankind at that time existed and lived like many modern educational books portray them as "cave people" grunting and drawing pictures upon cave walls!) Reality is populations gathered together would have been much more advanced in their thinking, in astrological matters, architectural, and machinery and in all technologies and Sciences of their time. Mankind who live in this world today know and understand things of this world in part because of advancements made since ancient biblical times as God has allowed.

Understanding the world and events according to the Bible is possible with God at the head but biblical events do not always coincide with worldly events and teachings which are of a different spirit. The Bible is the one true source of all things spiritual including Science and history since the world began God was.

Everything, because of sin, upon this earth is in a varying state of groaning, decay and decline; not advancing, as many highly educated persons in worldly affairs might purport today; this thinking is not based upon the spiritual truth of God's Word.

For we know that the whole creation groaneth and travaileth in pain together until now. (Romans 8:22 KJV)

Many ancient biblical chariots were developed to be elite wheels of their time; created to be fashionable and ornately decorated; but chiefly constructed to be highly functional in the heat of battle. Wood was a chief material used but advances in leather, iron, and other metals were utilized in manufacturing these "warrior carts" as this material was available based upon the location and technology of individual settlements or larger gatherings of a greater population could make more chariots more efficiently.

Chariots were always a picture or an outward expression of wealth and military strength. Some groups had much more ornate chariots, while others were much more unsophisticated rough around the edges and built crudely to serve in the battles at hand from what was readily available.

Much can be found in ancient history depicting chariots including those carved and drawn on walls in caves depicting scenes of battles throughout various societies of the biblical era. These drawings are also found in archeology and other ancient writings from historians of biblical times. These findings serve to further enhance our limited knowledge of this era of history; and especially how it compares to our living conditions and military battles today.

The compilation of chariots was not an easy task and the right resources were necessary for a society to accumulate enough for an army to proceed into battle upon. Chariot companies, like military groups formed today, were not common in early regimes unless they were a very resourceful and prosperous society. Solomon, for example, was very affluent and his battle ready army was top of the line and huge in size.

The Bible says:

And Solomon had forty thousand stalls of horses for his chariots, and twelve thousand horsemen. (1 Kings 4:26 KJV)

And Solomon had four thousand stalls for horses and chariots, and twelve thousand horsemen; whom he bestowed in the chariot cities, and with the king at Jerusalem. (2 Chronicles 9:25 KJV)

Many types of hand to hand combat weapons, including axes, spears, and bows were kept ready for the warrior who was atop the chariot in the heat of battles. The weapons used were quite primitive in comparison to today's modern and stealthily hidden armaments available enhancing the element of surprise.

The chariots were manufactured with available resources of the time period but not able to withstand the force of the wall of water held up by God's power at work in the Red Sea in protecting the Israelites crossing. After their successful journey across on the run from the

Egyptians, God allowed the stalled waters to be swept back powerfully into their natural place with a thundering potency. This force was said to easily break up chariots into many fragments which fell to the bottom of the Red Sea in at sea water burial all at the hands of a supernatural mighty God.

And what he did unto the army of Egypt, unto their horses, and to their chariots; how he made the water of the Red sea to overflow them as they pursued after you, and how the LORD hath destroyed them unto this day; (Deuteronomy 11:4 KJV)

FOR FURTHER CONTEMPLATION:

The Lord can conquer your foes with the same vengeance if you allow Him to fight all your battles; whether it is exploring great battle examples of ancient history on chariots or military vehicles of today; God is a God of victory in battle both of a physical and spiritual in nature.

Acts of Wavering Faith

The opposite of faith is doubt.

The Bible has many instances of people struggling with lack of faith and nagging doubt.

We always add distance between ourselves and God through harboring lack of faith in Him and His great promises.

Biblical examples of wavering faith include:

- Ishmael was born because of Abraham and Sara's both attempted to do God's work in man's way and understanding.

And Sarai said unto Abram, Behold now, the LORD hath restrained me from bearing: I pray thee, go in unto my maid; it may be that I may obtain children by her. And Abram hearkened to the voice of Sarai. (Genesis 16:2 KJV)

- Israelites could not enter into The Promised Land

But with whom was he grieved forty years? was it not with them that had sinned, whose carcases fell in the wilderness? And to whom sware he that they should not enter into his rest, but to them that believed not? So we see that they could not enter in because of unbelief. (Hebrews 3:17-19 KJV)

- Peter walking on water

And Peter answered him and said, Lord, if it be thou, bid me come unto thee on the water. And he said, Come. And when Peter was come down out of the ship, he walked on the water, to go to Jesus. ***But when he saw the wind boisterous, he was afraid; and beginning to sink, he cried, saying, Lord, save me. (Matthew 14:27-30 KJV)***

- Jesus could not do miracles in His hometown due to lack of faith among His own family

But Jesus said unto them, A prophet is not without honour, but in his own country, and among his own kin, and in his own house. And he could there do no mighty work, save that he laid his hands upon a few sick folk, and healed them. And he marveled because of their unbelief. And he went round about the villages, teaching. (Mark 6:4-6 KJV)

- Elijah's wavering faith

And he said, Go forth, and stand upon the mount before the LORD. And, behold, the LORD passed by, and a great and strong wind rent the mountains, and brake in pieces the rocks before the LORD; but the LORD was not in the wind: and after the wind an earthquake; but the LORD was not in the earthquake: and after the wind an earthquake; but the LORD was not in the earthquake: And after the earthquake a fire; but the LORD was not in the fire: and after the fire a still small voice. And it was so, when Elijah heard it, that he wrapped his face in his mantle, and went out, and stood in the entering in of the cave. And, behold, there came a voice unto him, and said, What doest thou here, Elijah? And he said, I have been very jealous for the LORD God of hosts: because the children of Israel have forsaken thy covenant, thrown down thine altars, and slain thy prophets with the sword; and I, even I only, am left; and they seek my life, to take it away. (1 Kings 19:11-14 KJV)

FOR FURTHER CONTEMPLATION:

Wavering faith and unbelief taking up residence in your mind will keep you from experiencing spiritual fullness and blessings God has planned for your life. Hand over situations to God to handle in your behalf standing upon faith in Him instead of wavering in your own doubt.

Behold There Came A Leper

When he was come down from the mountain, great multitudes followed him. And, behold, there came a leper and worshipped him, saying, Lord, if thou wilt, thou canst make me clean. And Jesus put forth his hand, and touched him, saying, I will; be thou clean. And immediately his leprosy was cleansed. (Matthew 8:1-3 KJV)

This leper, no doubt, came in response to great faith of truth heard with his spiritual ears which were tuned into the things of God.

So then faith cometh by hearing, and hearing by the word of God. (Romans 10:17 KJV)

God revealed to him spiritual knowledge of Jesus Christ. God was the only one who could truly cleanse this man and provide hope for his eternal future.

Under the terms Old Testament law, the leper was defiled, dishonored and in a state of uncleanness. However, a physician was not beckoned but instead cases of leprosy required a minister of spiritual power to cleanse the individual. Leprosy is not a physical illness; in ancient times or now, that any new-fangled medicine can cure in a week; but rather is a spiritual issue, only Jesus Christ has the holy prescription to cure.

He is a leprous man, he is unclean: the priest shall pronounce him utterly unclean; his plague is in his head. (Leviticus 13:44 KJV)

A leprous individual was shunned by society and made to live outside the gate of the city. Outside the gates was where the garbage and other outcast items were kept. The leprous individual was further enjoined to warn anyone who might venture near him, as he lay outside the gates, because of possible contamination from his horrid physical and spiritual contagious condition.

This leprous disease develops slowly; just a sin starts out small, then progresses and ferments. Leprosy is first deeply rooted in the bones and joints, essentially at first indiscernible to anyone but God until the distinguishing spots begin to appear outside the body on the skin. This is likened to the vile condition of the natural man's heart. This is who a man really is in the depths of his heart. This vileness increasingly trickles out progressing onto the external body, where others are also are able to easily recognize it. Gradually, these leprous spots can exist over the entire body as oozing and festering wounds, as their physical body slowly wastes away. The body essentially begins deteriorating, leading to both physical and spiritual death if not properly addressed.

Can you identify the utter condition of leprosy upon your own wretched body? It is existing but in a condition of a living death. Just as going to hell in eternity will be like the agonizing process of death without end forever; a leper lives in indescribable and traumatic misery which takes a heavy toll upon them both physically and spiritually while upon this earth.

For the leper in Matthew chapter 8, it was a hopeless predicament; nothing could be done, apart from God's supernatural miraculous intervention. God is still in the healing business allowing healing miracles to take place according to His will today.

The story of this leper who was spiritually bold in approaching Christ among throngs of people is one of the greatest examples saving faith. This is a vivid picture of Christ choosing to stop in His tracks humbly reaching out to this deprived man, tainted from sin, given freely given God's rich grace and mercy moving him from outside the gates of the city inside and into the a personal relationship with God for all eternity.

And we know that all things work together for good to them that love God, to them who are the called according to his purpose. (Romans 8:28 KJV)

FOR FURTHER CONTEMPLATION:

Has leprosy left its tell-tale marks upon your skin? Come to The One who can remove its marks permanently from your life.

A Hard Right Turn

Jesus answered and said unto him, Verily, verily, I say unto thee, except a man be born again, he cannot see the kingdom of God. (John 3:3 KJV)

Jesus makes a powerful statement: "Unless one is born again, he cannot see the kingdom of God." "See" is an important word to grasp and hold onto in this verse.

One could assume a visual, literal observation of the Kingdom is at hand. However, in the Greek it actually means to know, to be aware of, or grasping onto a mental picture in lieu of an actual visual sighting.

The Kingdom of God is to be spiritually grasped in the mind of those who have turned their attention towards the things of Jesus Christ having been forgiven of personal sin quickened spiritually alive, or personally saved by faith in Jesus Christ. His kingdom includes a promise of a future eternal state with God forever.

Do you need to make a hard right turn upon the avenue which includes an eternal future? Will the Kingdom of Heaven be at the end of your spiritual journey, or eternal burning fires of hell, evil darkness, and suffering forever from spiritual thirst that cannot be quenched?

FOR FURTHER CONTEMPLATION:

Do you have full assurance of a heavenly eternal future or are doubts and questions concerning your eternal future filling your mind and heart turn your attention towards the things of God.

A Peculiar People

But ye are a chosen generation, a royal priesthood, an holy nation, a peculiar people; that ye should shew forth the praises of him who hath called you out of darkness into his marvellous light: (1 Peter 2:9 KJV)

For thou art an holy people unto the LORD thy God, and the LORD hath chosen thee to be a peculiar people unto himself, above all the nations that are upon the earth. (Deuteronomy 14:2 KJV)

For the LORD hath chosen Jacob unto himself, and Israel for his peculiar treasure. (Psalms 135:4 KJV)

Who gave himself for us, that he might redeem us from all iniquity, and purify unto himself a peculiar people, zealous of good works. (Titus 2:14KJV)

And ye shall not walk in the manners of the nation, which I cast out before you: for they committed all these things, and therefore I abhorred them. But I have said unto you, Ye shall inherit their land, and I will give it unto you to possess it, a land that floweth with milk and honey: I am the LORD your God, which have separated you from other people. (Leviticus 20:23-24KJV)

The Lord has set His sheep or the Jewish people apart and grafted in, or included the Gentiles, into His spiritual fold. God set aside His spiritual family as His peculiar people. They are to live, sojourning not dwelling as pilgrims and strangers upon this earth. We are set aside as His possession or "spiritual flock" of sheep and Jesus Christ is our Good Shepherd as we live in the fields of life. He places us in His sheepfold as night and darkness roll in hedging about us a wall of rocks and boulders, keeping us in His sight, protecting us, and caring for us as He loves us unconditionally.

Jesus Christ, The Good Shepherd loves His sheep, and unlike a hired servant or shepherd might; He never will flee from our side and if wolves gather about us with the sole intention of harming us He lovingly set a hedge about us, implying His spiritual ownership of us. We are truly special, peculiar, and set aside in His eyes now and for all eternity.

The holy and unconditional love and care He provides for us brings an awesome accountability into our court. We are a unique possession an earthly picture of God in heaven. We are imperfect, He is flawless and perfection.

Wherefore henceforth know we no man after the flesh: yea, though we have known Christ after the flesh, yet now henceforth know we him no more. Therefore if any man be in Christ, he is a new creature: old things are passed away; behold, all things are become new. (2 Corinthians 5:16-17 KJV)

An unapologetic Christian does not capitulate to society's popular whims and beliefs. A Christian never strives to "fit in" with the popular crowd, or the opinion of man, or bestowing upon themselves the latest popular fashion trends of the world looking and sounding like mankind who is lost and dying in this world.

However, we also are not endeavoring to set ourselves apart from the world and from God, making a name for ourselves by following a set of personally held strict beliefs or a standard of "religiosity" we lawfully adhere to.

The belief structure of all true disciples of Jesus Christ always point to God and Jesus Christ and the Holy Spirit and is laid solely upon the foundation of His holy Biblical scriptures not upon the whims and beliefs of any false manmade religion.

We are to live a consistent life of who we are in Him, not of who we are apart from Him. He is always the object of our hope, faith, and belief. He is the promise, seal, and hope of our redemption. He paid our sin debt we could never afford.

FOR FURTHER CONTEMPLATION:

Our eternal future is sealed upon the promises of God and completed through the sacrifices of Jesus Christ on the cross. We are always striving for His glory and recognition, not ours.

All about Hell

Noble soul winning includes discussion about horrible conditions waiting in Hell for lost souls. Those individuals who do not freely accept God's gift of salvation through faith, while living on earth, will never have any opportunity for peace and eternal life in Heaven and for continuously glorifying God. Instead, they will discover, immediately at the moment of their death, they are permanent residents of a ghastly dark ghetto of constant agony and torment called Hell.

In the deep pit of Hell inhabitants have a vivid memory that never fails to recall lost opportunities for salvation, turning points in life that were ignored, forks in the road where wrong choices were made. This memory will incessantly haunt and disturb lost souls serving to revive horrible sins and situations which characterized their careless and hell bent life upon this earth.

Requests and appeals will be deprived in Hell. Basic human needs and comfort such as hunger and, thirst, mercy and rest, which most have had met or abundantly exceeded while sojourning upon this earth, will be flat out denied in Hell.

The next time you are complaining about the heat while in the midst of comfortable air conditioning on earth, imagine how hot and uncomfortable the torment of Hell will be for eternity for all lost souls.

And there was a certain beggar named Lazarus, which was laid at his gate, full of sores, And desiring to be fed with the crumbs which fell from the rich man's table: moreover the dogs came and licked his sores. And it came to pass, that the beggar died, and was carried by the angels into Abraham's bosom: the rich man also died, and was buried; And in hell he lift up his eyes, being in torments, and seeth Abraham afar off, and Lazarus in his bosom. And he cried and said, Father Abraham, have mercy on me, and send Lazarus, that he may dip the tip of his finger in water, and cool my tongue; for I am tormented in this flame. But Abraham

said, Son, remember that thou in thy lifetime receivedst thy good things, and likewise Lazarus evil things: but now he is comforted, and thou art tormented. (Luke 16:20-25KJV)

For Further Contemplation:

Where will you be residing for all eternity? In the flames and fires of Hell; or amid the peace which surrounds Jesus Christ upon the heavenly throne?

Until the Robe Adorns You

And they crucified him, and parted his garments, casting lots: that it might be fulfilled which was spoken by the prophet, They parted my garments among them, and upon my vesture did they cast lots. (Matthew 27:35 KJV)

He clothed us from head to foot with garments of spiritual fortitude and sturdy battle ready armor. He was put to death on the cross as a common criminal so that we could be adorned in His glorious garments of royalty. Jesus hung naked on the cross, while men divided His clothes by lot, so that we could rest in spiritual peace arrayed in His fine and holy garments.

Many who profess to be Christians have since given up their fight against their old nature and are white knuckled and desperately clinging to their old filthy garments, and doing whatever seems right in their own eyes.

Do not defile His holy garments with stains of sin; that is a spiritual insult unto the holiness of God.

FOR FURTHER CONTEMPLATION:

Let your garment always be white. You will never spiritually rest until He has clothed you with His finest robe of royalty, deposited your confessed sin into the deepest sea, adopting you into His spiritual family.

The Test of Fire

But he knoweth the way that I take: when he hath tried me, I shall come forth as gold. (Job 23:10 KJV)

Fire is important for mankind. It can be hurtful or harmful depending upon circumstances at hand. All individuals have a working knowledge of the impact of fire in our lives in some fashion; from campfires to cooking; enjoying the warmth and comfort fire provides taking away chill in the air; the making of food, to the harsh and destructive heat it can produce developing into a fiery inferno of a friendly blaze gone awry leading to certain destruction and loss.

God applies the perfect touch of fire upon our lives as He deems necessary to bring about His will in our life.

Fire has many godly uses in our life:

Fire warms us up when the temperatures drop outside and fire heats and cooks our food as meal time approaches. Without fire to keep us warm and dry and full. Physical life would not be able sustainable in this world without certain elements including fire.

Not only does fire keep our living conditions tolerable and pleasant but it can serve to wake us; warning us of unpleasant situations or danger lurking ahead. This "friendly" variety of fire can burn and chafe; often leaving a mark or scar that is useful in stirring us from our spiritual slumber. All Christians including, you and I, take naps on the job from time to time. On occasion some may fall into a deeper slumber; even turning their face from God like the prodigal son mentioned in the book of Luke.

Fire can purge or eliminate sticks, beams and toothpicks in our eyes and melt away hidden impurities, and afflictions in our life. Fire burns away weeds and prickly thorns choking our spiritual desire and intruding or preventing further progress along His narrow path; according to His will for our life.

The apostle Paul had a thorn in his side of some sort and God chose to leave it in place rather than remove it; allowing its placement in his life to strengthen his reserve and spiritual fortitude as he continued to walk hand in hand with God upon this earth.

Fire thrust upon our lives often serves to illuminate sin in our life; thrusting a yellow caution flag or warning in our face regarding the condition of our spiritual health. This is a heat or fire in our life that should stop us in our tracks causing us to take a second look at the circumstances surrounding us and the direction we are headed.

Fire warms our heart; providing a blazing heat for our spiritual comfort, but can also impact us with blistering temperatures; moving us along the path if God deems we need to progress farther, going from milk to meat, on our spiritual journey.

Fire smolders, sometimes for hours or days, with even the smallest or finest embers receiving the necessary elements of the fire triangle to keep it slowly but purposely smoldering its way to becoming a full-blown fire.

God never gives up easily when we try to ignore or smother His holy fire burning within us. His Spirit keeps stirring the pot within us to revitalize the flames as a blaring reminder of changes He deems necessary for our spiritual equilibrium and symmetry in our life.

Fire has many godly uses as it permeates all the senses. Fire can be seen, heard, felt, and touched; affecting all areas of our life as we endure or battle the spiritual blazes roaring with all of us.

If you are not living a life filled with joy you are living beneath the spiritual pleasure and privilege God intends for your life. God will not hesitate to start a holy fire to get you moving in His will. God will also use fire for refining you in some way; removing silt and impurities and making you a vessel useful for carrying out His plans for your life.

FOR FURTHER CONTEMPLATION:

He will wholly consume you; purifying your life as necessary for carrying out His will and way. Are you spiritually available for His holy direction? If not, He will get your attention by turning up the heat underneath you as you sojourn upon this earth.

A City without Walls

He that hath no rule over his own spirit is like a city that is broken down, and without walls. (Proverbs 25:28 KJV)

God's original plan for man was that He controls the world and through Him man controls himself. Since the time of the first couple, Adam and Eve, man has not been successful in governing his own actions and physical body, proving himself to be undisciplined and disorderly in a world filled with temptations and many opportunities not always from the hands of God but from the god of this world.

In ancient times city walls were a first line defense of the city. The city walls protected treasures inside the city, just as self-control and self-government protects one from falling overboard into habitual sin and personal destruction; outside of the will of God in life.

Jesus Christ allows us to be disciplined in mind, soul, spirit, and our physical body when living through His power and control in our life. He keeps the wall surrounding us in sound repair. Man, on the other hand, left alone to His devices, is always hovering just a step away from certain disaster.

Daniel is a prime example of a Biblical character that had the resolve, through Jesus Christ, to live a life of order and obedience and remaining steadfast in the things of God.

I ate no pleasant bread, neither came flesh nor wine in my mouth, neither did I anoint myself at all, till three whole weeks were fulfilled. (Daniel 10:3 KJV)

Daniel purposed in his heart, at the beginning of his captivity as a teenager, to be obedient to God and flatly refusing a seat at the king's table feasting upon rich and royal food. Near the end of his life, approximately age 90, in chapter ten of Daniel, he remains tenacious and steadfastly resolved to uphold his beliefs in God and continuing to live a spirit controlled life.

Daniel mourned and fasted for three weeks in order to communicate spiritually and intimately with God. Because Daniel was obedient and spiritually available to God this allowed God to work and direct his path through life. God was able to use him in comprehending prophecy and properly interpreting the king's dreams.

Can God use your life to further His kingdom? How much control does the Holy Spirit have over your life? Are you standing firm behind His wall of first line defense in your life? Or is your life out of control, unfocused spiritually towards Him and captive instead to the things of the god of this world instead?

FOR FURTHER CONTEMPLATION:

Allow His Holy spirit to build a fortress around your life so you can be successful in fulfilling the purposes He has for you.

A Humble and Useful Vessel Mete for Christ

For this thing I besought the Lord thrice, that it might depart from me. And he said unto me, My grace is sufficient for thee: for my strength is made perfect in weakness. Most gladly therefore will I rather glory in my infirmities, that the power of Christ may rest upon me. Therefore I take pleasure in infirmities, in reproaches, in necessities, in persecutions, in distresses for Christ's sake: for when I am weak, then am I strong. (2 Corinthians 12:8-10 KJV)

Most will not be forced to die at the stake, stoned and left to die, executed at short range, endure lashings, hang helplessly in the gallows, or be imprisoned for preaching about the Lord Jesus Christ.

Persecution in the United States is not an issue most Christians endure as those in other countries do for their faith in Christ. We are freely able to choose to attend church, openly witness, and hand out tracts, preach the Word, and live a life of truth in obedience to His Word.

God's grace is sufficient for whatever situation we are in the midst of. It is ultimately in His strength that we exist and function, not in our own power and purpose. His grace is more than sufficient to meet our immediate need. His grace is always abundant, over and above what the task at hand entails and always leads to His glory and honor not to any of our own.

Now unto him that is able to do exceeding abundantly above all that we ask or think, according to the power that worketh in us, Unto him be glory in the church by Christ Jesus throughout all ages, world without end. Amen. (Ephesians 3:20-21)

Times of weakness and spiritual need perfect our humbleness, purging out prideful tendencies and willful propensities to follow our own path in accomplishing a desired outcome.

We are troubled on every side, yet not distressed; we are perplexed, but not in despair; Persecuted, but not forsaken; cast down, but not destroyed; Always bearing about in the body the dying of the Lord Jesus, that the life also of Jesus might be made manifest in our body. (2 Corinthians 4:8-10 KJV)

My Yoke is Easy

Come unto me, all ye that labour and are heavy laden, and I will give you rest. Take my yoke upon you, and learn of me; for I am meek and lowly in heart: and ye shall find rest unto your souls. For my yoke is easy, and my burden is light. (Matthew 11:28-30KJV)

A yoke is an ancient harness used to yoke, or put together or unite a pair of working animals, usually oxen or horses. This uniting together helped to spread the workload into two equal portions neither animal bearing the full weight of the load.

We are like an ox, tugging and pulling at our hefty workload of church, family, careers, and such, stopping only occasionally to wipe the sweat off our brow dragging a vast pile of important work or obligations alongside us as we move about in this hectic and busy world. Not moving at a snail's pace but rather at the devil's hurried and frantic pace. It is like having a ball and chain wrapped around our ankle as we try to run in haste.

The Lord calls unto us to come. **"Come unto me all that labour…"** Some hear His voice beckoning while others choose to ignore God's call and continue marching along in the chaotic parade of this world tuning out the call of God upon their life.

Others find themselves stopped at a crossroad and feeling burdensome with an ever-present load of trouble weighing them down until they are literally crawling along at a snail's pace. Hearing God's voice bidding to them to come and simply reach out for His yoke sounds so comforting and pleasant to their tired ears. God calls: **"Come unto me, all ye that labour and are heavy laden, and I will give you rest…"**

His yoke upon us, what could that possibly mean? To the world it sounds burdensome, heavy, and confining. It sounds like His yoke would restrain us from living life to the fullest.

Nothing could be further from the truth. His yoke is a one on one personal relationship with Him. It connects us directly to Him. Seeing our helpless condition before Him and confessing our sin puts God squarely in the driver's seat of our life. This means He is sharing in our burdens and trials.

Instead of the impediment of our sin and burdens dragging us to the ground He invites us to lay them upon His broad encompassing shoulders, lifting us up. We are harnessed together, or yoked together with Him harnessing the weight.

And as they led him away, they laid hold upon one Simon, a Cyrenian, coming out of the country, and on him they laid the cross, that he might bear it after Jesus. (Luke 23:26 KJV)

Simon of Cyrene was asked to bear Jesus Christ's burden of carrying the cross towards the hill of death and torture on Calvary. Jesus Christ will come along side us, if we seek Him and pray, bearing our overwhelming burdens too.

God says:

"His yoke is easy and His burdens are light…"

Living for Jesus Christ and shining in His holy spiritual parade is living a life filled to overflowing with His inner peace and joy. It is a refreshing life. Gone are the weights that so easily beset us, overwhelm us, and knock us down.

Be careful for nothing; but in every thing by prayer and supplication with thanksgiving let your requests be

made known unto God. And the peace of God, which passeth all understanding, shall keep your hearts and minds through Christ Jesus. (Philippians 4:6-7 KJV)

FOR FURTHER CONTEMPLATION:

Are you crawling around overburdened with sins and cares riding upon your shoulder? His yoke is light and easy.

Seek Not To Be Loosed

So ought men to love their wives as their own bodies. He that loveth his wife loveth himself. For no man ever yet hated his own flesh; but nourisheth and cherisheth it, even as the Lord the church: For we are members of his body, of his flesh, and of his bones. For this cause shall a man leave his father and mother, and shall be joined unto his wife, and they two shall be one flesh. (Ephesians 5:28-31 KJV)

War has been declared on marriage. One dilemma of modern – day marriage is the ease and societal acceptance of divorce as the first sign of struggle and strife rears its ugly head.

Art thou bound unto a wife? seek not to be loosed. Art thou loosed from a wife? seek not a wife. (1 Corinthians 7:27 KJV)

The other assault on marriage today is that it is being redefined, redefined by those who agree to the terms of "living together," having no lasting promise or commitment towards each other. It is also being redefined as union between two men or two women. Since the beginning God has always defined marriage as a union between a Man and a Woman. The Family is made up of a Man and a Woman, and their offspring. A Family never consists of two men and their offspring, nor can it be two women and their offspring. The only way man can naturally multiply and replenish the earth, a directive of God, is a union between a man and a woman.

So God created man in his own image, in the image of God created he him; male and female created he them. And God blessed them, and God said unto them, Be fruitful, and multiply, and replenish the earth, and subdue it: and have dominion over the fish of the sea, and over the fowl of the air, and over every living thing that moveth upon the earth. (Genesis 1:27-28 KJV)

To make your marriage endure through hard times look to God first, then choose purposely to live every day as if you were still your honeymoon. Look for those small opportunities each day to love your spouse in the small events of life. It will never be the anniversary celebrations, huge diamonds or flowers that make a marriage special. It will be how one lives married to their spouse each and every day that makes a marriage priceless and enduring through any rough patches in life.

Strife does rear its ugly head in every relationship. We are all human and are subject to pride and selfishness from time to time. The strife you have is with God with the fault lying squarely in your corner. Strife occurs when you have moved to the left or right and are out of holy agreement with God. God has not called us to come into agreement with others, He's called us to be in agreement with Him and His scripture, as we agree with God all other relationships will fall into their proper place. This important truth can solve a lot of common marriage issues. The strife that comes to the surface in our marriage relationship between one another needs to be dealt with by getting our own hearts right with God first and foremost. Nothing will be solved until your relationship with God is in order.

God is a God of love. Love covers or blankets over a multitude of sin and strife. Loving others with an unconditional love; no matter the circumstances at hand is following the example of love as Christ loved us while we were yet sinners.

Charity suffereth long, and is kind; charity envieth not; charity vaunteth not itself, is not puffed up, Doth not behave itself unseemly, seeketh not her own, is not easily provoked, thinketh no evil; Rejoiceth not in iniquity, but rejoiceth in the truth; Beareth all things,

believeth all things, hopeth all things, endureth all things. (1 Corinthians 13:4-7 KJV)

The covenant I made at the altar was with God as well as with my spouse. Only God can give you the necessary strength and endurance to love your spouse when he or she is unlovable. It is choosing to love without strings attached. This is opposite of how the world loves or values marriage. In a world-centered view, many will sustain marriage vows only as long as our own comforts, desires, contentment, and expectations are being met.

I can choose to see marriage as God views it:

- ❖ To forgive my spouse for forgetting my birthday or anniversary or other special occasions.
- ❖ To be merciful and gracious when my spouse makes a mistake
- ❖ To not to hold grudges.
- ❖ To forgive my spouse for unfaithfulness; whether it be spiritual or physical in nature.
- ❖ To not to compare him/her to other spouses or other relationships.

The relationship between Christ and the church primarily, and secondly the marital relationship as it was between Aquila and Priscilla are solid biblical examples for Christian husbands and wives to strive to mirror in their own marriage.

Aquila and Priscilla's names are always mentioned together in scripture. Marriages cannot be fine-tuned and in working order if couples do not *purposely* choose to spend time together building upon their relationship. Somewhere between ordinary tasks that often fill our days such as taking out the garbage, paying bills, cleaning house, mowing the lawn, disciplining the kids, folding the laundry… all the everyday routines of life is where couples often easily loose the "honeymoon" atmosphere of their marriage; replacing it with many ordinary or ho hum responsibilities found in every day cares of the world. Spiritual tweaking must be incorporated into every marriage and be fine-tuned often according to God's scale not according to the world's loose standards for optimum spiritual connection between God and each spouse coming together in the marriage triangle.

FOR FURTHER CONTEMPLATION:

A successful marriage requires godly commitment and spiritual endurance. The marriage union cannot be accomplished in man's own strength, without God being placed at the top of the marriage triangle, in proper spiritual order and rightful place. An earthly marriage is a picture of Christ and the church it is a serious undertaking intended for a lifetime.

Hath God Said…?

Now the serpent was more subtil than any beast of the field which the LORD God had made. And he said unto the woman, Yea, hath God said, Ye shall not eat of every tree of the garden? (Genesis 3:1 KJV)

Satan caused Eve to doubt what God had said in the Garden of Eden. Satan is still up to his cunning tricks and deception causing a downward spiral of doubt and uncertainty to clutter minds toward things of God. God's Word says He has given us a mind that can be focused, reliable, and temperate as we wade through this spiritual and mind-boggling jungle upon this earth.

For God hath not given us the spirit of fear; but of power, and of love, and of a sound mind. (2 Timothy 1:7 KJV)

"Hath God said…?"   This seemingly insignificant query is actually very important to our spiritual well-being. Doubt begs mankind to question the authenticity and authority of God. Seeds of doubt harvest confusion dividing our mind towards all things of God. Like a spiritual cancer doubt creeps in to our minds unaware at first; like an earthworm it wiggles and muscles itself burrowing deeper and deeper into our patterns and habits until it vastly permeates our mind-set creating a web of deception. This web infuses together spiritual beliefs; "religious" views of the Eastern and Western world, traditions of man, psychology, holistic healing, astrology, self-help, science and many other "religious" agendas always with self as the backbone or pillar these temporary solutions ultimately rest upon. The authority of God and beliefs based upon His Word are often labeled as old-fashioned and out of context to the reality of today's world as God is placed upon the shelf along with many other gods.

Once this deceptive web, begun to be spun with Eve, downplaying the authority of God and the Truth of His Word they are no longer recognizable or distinguishable to many caught in this self-willed and self-driven cockeyed belief system. It is no longer about the authority, holiness, and justice of God. Rather it is about living life without walls or limits. Do what is right in your own eyes and find your own way or walk down the path that feels right to you. Live your own life with a positive outlook and believe you are a good person who is on the right path and doing the best that you can do as you exist in this world. This belief system, based solely upon a defective foundation of man, places the existence of the authority of God on the back burner to simmer.

God has commandments, precepts, limits, and righteous judgment for all mankind; whether man chooses to acknowledge God living for Him or following the gods of this world.

God set forth in the New Testament through the preaching of Paul that those who chose to follow after Him would be living sold out lives to Him and His will for their life; not living unto self:

I beseech you therefore, brethren, by the mercies of God, that ye present your bodies a living sacrifice, holy, acceptable unto God, which is your reasonable service. And be not conformed to this world: but be ye transformed by the renewing of your mind, that ye may prove what is that good, and acceptable, and perfect, will of God. (Romans 12:1-2 KJV)

He does chastise His own spiritual family as they live and learn within the divine protection of His spiritual safety net which is infused with love, mercy and grace.

Ultimately all mankind will answer to Him. Man has been given free will to choose to live in faith towards the authority of God in their life or choosing to live their life according to their own authority. God will never force Himself upon anyone but allows all men to choose to follow Him.

Solomon learned that all things happening today also happened throughout history:

The thing that hath been, it is that which shall be; and that which is done is that which shall be done: and there is no new thing under the sun. (Ecclesiastes 1:9 KJV)

Solomon was alluding to the fact that history always repeats itself. Alarming or eye opening things happening in this world today have already happened in the past. Biblically based precepts teach there is no really no such thing as a New Age Movement but rather old deceptive beliefs from the god of this world recycling or being repurposed in and out of popularity and social acceptance as the times and man waver and change.

The Bible definitively tells us God and His precepts never change:

Jesus Christ the same yesterday, and to day, and for ever. (Hebrews 13:8 KJV)

The cycle of wickedness and evil from those who are living in enmity against the holy things of God and choosing to live for self, changes with the wind. The Apostle Paul tells us in the book of Second Timothy that clever deceptions, wickedness will become worse and worse throughout the ages:

Yea, and all that will live godly in Christ Jesus shall suffer persecution. But evil men and seducers shall wax worse and worse, deceiving, and being deceived. But continue thou in the things which thou hast learned and hast been assured of, knowing of whom thou hast learned them; And that from a child thou hast known the holy scriptures, which are able to make thee wise unto salvation through faith which is in Christ Jesus. (2 Timothy 3:12-15 KJV)

This verse also gives the spiritual man the answer to living amidst the many deceptive situations at hand. **"Continue in the things which thou has learned..."** The men of God should continue in God's Word following Him as He glides us through the muck of this world pulling us along and carrying us as it is necessary for our spiritual well-being.

If you do not have a personal relationship with God then today is the perfect time to meet Him personally through faith in His Son Jesus Christ and allow Him to infuse His righteousness into you and claim salvation in Him for your soul.

(For he saith, I have heard thee in a time accepted, and in the day of salvation have I succoured thee: behold, now is the accepted time; behold, now is the day of salvation.) (2 Corinthians 6:2 KJV)

FOR FURTHER CONTEMPLATION:

It is never too late to pry off the web of trickery and deception from its hold on your mind allowing God's Word to permeate your whole being and trickle down into your dry and thirsty heart for now and for all eternity.

Spiritual Adoption

For ye have not received the spirit of bondage again to fear; but ye have received the Spirit of adoption, whereby we cry, Abba, Father. The Spirit itself beareth witness with our spirit, that we are the children of God: (Romans 8:15-16 KJV)

A paramount spiritual transaction, THE ULTIMATE SACRIFICE of God and His only begotten Son, took place when Jesus Christ died upon the cross shedding His precious blood as payment in full for all sin: past, present, and future over two thousand years ago. His death on Calvary was the transaction and His resurrection from the grave three days later completed this spiritual reckoning; bringing about a holy remedy of adoption into the eternal spiritual family of God for those who placed their faith in God through Jesus Christ.

Individuals who continue to live in sin, by choice, live in bondage to sin and under the weight and authority of the law. Those who choose to live in faith through Jesus Christ, choose the narrow path, and are lead to eternity bound by God's grace. This grace God extends to us is undeserved favor because of our sin nature, and paid for by Jesus Christ's death upon the cross. This unmerited favor frees us from our sin debt. Therefore, we go from bondage and a harsh task master; to freedom through Jesus Christ and a personal relationship with God.

A relationship with Jesus Christ removes us from our spiritual desert, our Babylon, or our land of Egypt; placing us in spiritual fullness in the land of milk and honey where the waters flow and even seasons of fiery trials and tribulations flow with inner joy indescribable as we march onward towards eternity.

Whosoever places their faith in His Son Jesus Christ become adopted sons of God's spiritual family. Adopted sons and daughters are placed, or grafted in the spiritual family of God. Both His Son, who sits at His right hand, and adopted sons and daughters have fellowship with God now; and for all eternity.

It is important to note the transaction of adopting a child is a legal and binding agreement. Just like parents who choose to adopt a child legally become the child's parents; when adopted in God's family we acknowledge God as our spiritual parent repenting, or change their mind about our own personal sin, placing faith in Jesus Christ, acknowledging on a personal level the transaction Jesus Christ completed, or finished, at the cross for payment of all sin; past, present, and future.

This spiritual transaction is complete . There is nothing that can be added, subtracted, or altered in this equation. It is not like placing an order at a home improvement store for flooring; then changing your mind about some detail of the color or craftsmanship and choosing to switch to another product before the flooring project is laid. Likewise a family would not adopt a child whom they promise to love and cherish and later contact the adoption agency with the sole intent of giving back the child because he or she is imperfect in some way. No, parents operating upon Christian principals and precepts would accept any child as a creation of God; loving it unconditionally despite any cracks, fissures or warts.

In whom ye also trusted, after that ye heard the word of truth, the gospel of your salvation: in whom also after that ye believed, ye were sealed with that holy Spirit of promise, (Ephesians 1:13 KJV)

When a person comes to God in faith through His Son the deal is sealed. The Holy Spirit seals the individual; placing him in the safety of God's nail scarred hands, preserving him and wrapping him in the unconditional blanket of God's love and righteousness with an unconditional promise of eternal life.

Being wrapped up in God's holy seal preserves men from any intrusion attempt or fleshly appeal to break this divine seal or impression the Holy Spirit has placed upon every believer's life. Individuals who have salvation through Jesus Christ are sealed and impenetrable making them steadfast and unmovable against any outside sources. The devil and his minions can detect this sealing, or setting aside, upon a believer's life. This peculiarity emits a wonderful stream of spiritual fragrance flowing from the believer's inner soul; softened and captivated by the things of God; flowing outwards to any person in their midst.

And I give unto them eternal life; and they shall never perish, neither shall any man pluck them out of my hand. My Father, which gave them me, is greater than all; and no man is able to pluck them out of my Father's hand. (John 10:28-29 KJV)

This verse is in the present tense: I give. God gives us that seal immediately upon salvation identifying our position within His spiritual kingdom. This designates our spiritual standing; that we are no longer our own; but bought with the price of His Sons shed blood and kept unconditionally with God for eternity. God continues to give and give and give beyond the seal of salvation to His adopted spiritual family who may be "good" according to the world's standards; according to God's commandments and precepts deserve nothing less than to burn in the fires of Hell. Despite our innate sin nature and many shortcomings He gives His own family unconditional love; joy unspeakable, beauty for ashes, grace abounding, peace that passeth understanding, and new mercies every morning.

By far, the best gift of all is His gift of eternal life to whosoever believes and has a change of mind about their individual sin and the holiness and authority of God. Nothing can come between God and His adopted spiritual family once a believer is placed by God in His nail scarred hand, cloaked with a white robe, and enveloped in His unconditional love.

For I am persuaded, that neither death, nor life, nor angels, nor principalities, nor powers, nor things present, nor things to come, Nor height, nor depth, nor any other creature, shall be able to separate us from the love of God, which is in Christ Jesus our Lord. (Romans 8:38-39 KJV)

No event, present or future, or in Heaven or Hell can keep us from receiving God's love. The past, present and our entire future are wrapped up in the love of Jesus Christ. We can have complete and absolute assurance of our salvation and eternal life.

These things have I written unto you that believe on the name of the Son of God; that ye may know that ye have eternal life, and that ye may believe on the name of the Son of God. (1 John 5:13 KJV)

We do not hope for a future in Heaven with God. Or guess that we will be in Heaven with God. We do not need to continually pray that we will end up in Heaven with God. Or work for a chance at spending eternity with God. Never do we just think we might end up in eternity with God.

We can absolutely KNOW FOR SURE we will be with God and Jesus Christ forever, now and in eternity, because we have placed our faith in His Son, Jesus Christ, accepting God's free gift of salvation for whosoever believes and been adopted into His spiritual family.

For Further Contemplation:

You can know where you will spend all eternity.

The Three Triune God

I will **pray** says the **son** (intercession)

I will **send** says the **Father** (bestowment)

I will **comfort** says the **Holy Spirit** (that is supernatural peace)

Trinity was designed by the Father, bought by the life-giving blood of His Son, and protected, or sealed, by the workings of Holy Spirit. It is a down-payment of Heaven upon this earth for whosoever will grasp onto this triune relationship, a foundation firmly planted in love with God, while living in this world amongst much wickedness and darkness.

The real spiritual baptism is done by the Holy Spirit inside a person's heart. He takes a heart of stone softened by His Word and fills it with His Spirit, creating a pliable heart ready for His will and way. The Baptism of the local church is a portrait of the Holy Spirit's work inside us and our newness of life in the Spirit.

Let's focus upon each separate and intrinsic member of the Trinity for a moment. As best we can comprehend, with our finite minds, while living here on earth:

What did our redemption cost **God the Father**?

God – He was willing to sacrifice His only begotten son. The death of His Son on Calvary cost god all that He had. This was an extreme cost for a father to undergo for the benefit of mankind. God the Father could see the hatred and disdain of man towards His son firsthand, God could feel the extreme suffering His Son felt as He hung upon that old rugged cross, and God was in extreme agony Himself as His son said:

When Jesus therefore had received the vinegar, he said, It is finished: and he bowed his head, and gave up the ghost. (John 19:30 KJV)

This was the moment the three triune God was separated: Father spiritually apart from His Son and His Son separated from His Father. The immense and excruciating pain and despondency felt at that moment was indeed almost unbearable.

Praise the Lord the biblical account does not end here we serve a risen Savior who supernaturally arose from sting of death and His grave on the third day, just as was prophesied spiritually joining together in life those who man separated by physical death in this world.

What did the redemption cost **Jesus** His Son?

Jesus- who before His incarnation had never known pain, never stepped upon a briar, never was familiar with the shivers of cold, or the pangs of hunger, fatigue or deprivation of any kind; was willing to be made into flesh by the Father and come to earth. He had never been subject to life, as we know it, existing on earth. He had never felt the limitations or pain of a human body. He had never been without the Spirit residing inside of Him. He had never known or heard mocking or ridicule, only Heaven's joyful hymns, worship and exaltation. In the realms of glory His "parentage" or lineage was never brought into question or challenged in any way. He had never been lonely or felt despair. He never felt abandoned and was never without the fellowship of the Trinity or the adoration of angels. His motives had never been questioned. His words had never been doubted. In fact, He was the very Word of God in the flesh.

What did the redemption cost the **Holy Spirit**:

The Holy Spirit was quenched. The sting of sin, the entire sin debt of all men, was placed upon Jesus as He hung upon the cross. This sin debt was staggering, a debt nobody but the Son of God could repay. This debt was so looming and massive it quenched the Holy Spirit as the moment Jesus said "It is finished."

The Holy Spirit was without breath, or life, at that very moment in time. The Spirit is the comforter, instructor holy guide; He quickens, and intercedes for us with the Father, even when we do not have our own words to articulate prayerful conversation with Him. The Holy Spirit was not in any communication with the Father, on Jesus's behalf, at this very moment of His physical death.

Praise the Lord Jesus won the victory over death. Jesus did arise from His grave three days later securing victory over death and breathing new life into the Holy Spirit which then ascended upon Jesus Christ at Pentecost. This completed the eternal path for whosoever believeth on the three triune God; Father, Son, and Holy Spirit.

In the beginning was the Word, and the Word was with God, and the Word was God. The same was in the beginning with God. (John 1:1-2 KJV)

And the Word was made flesh, and dwelt among us, (and we beheld his glory, the glory as of the only begotten of the Father,) full of grace and truth. (John 1:14 KJV)

I am Alpha and Omega, the beginning and the end, the first and the last. (Revelation 22:13 KJV)

There is no spiritual good in the earth of which the three triune God; Father, Son, and Holy Spirit is not the author, creator and sustainer. He was there in the beginning of time and will be present at the ending of time. Those who expediently obey His will, leading, and power receive the things of God; whatever it may He has in store for our lives.

When Christians choose to be disobedient to the will of God and sow unspiritual fruits into our lives we can quench or limit ourselves from the Spirit of God working within us. Sin of any sort separates us from God, creating a ravine between us and Him, just as it came between God and His Sn Jesus hanging upon the cross. The three triune God is holy and sin never resides within Him. His power can keep us upon the path towards Christ-likeness as we journey towards eternity.

And grieve not the holy Spirit of God, whereby ye are sealed unto the day of redemption. Let all bitterness, and wrath, and anger, and clamor, and evil speaking, be put away from you, with all malice: And be ye kind one to another, tender-hearted, forgiving one another, even as God for Christ's sake hath forgiven you. (Ephesians 4:30-32 KJV)

Oh that we may never grieve, or quench the fire of, the Holy Spirit but rather obey, praise and adore Him. He wants to express Himself in and through our attitudes and actions; reaping a harvest of spiritual fruits bringing Him glory and honor. We hinder His spirit by living in a sinful lifestyle and not separating ourselves apart from the world unto the Father's will for our lives.

Sometimes we choose to lead our lives without including God in the blueprint going out on a dangerous and crooked path that "feels right" according to our feeling, emotions, and standards the world has set forth for us to stumble down upon the wider path leading to Hell.

Not including Him in every fine detail of our lives outwardly declares we can handle things on our own and in our own way. Equivocally this is stating we know better than God and essentially are looking for a vacancy in the trinity, allowing us to rule and govern our own life just as we please, leaving God out of the picture.

FOR FURTHER CONTEMPLATION:

The three triune holy God has everything under His control since the beginning of time. Allow Him to steer you in His supernatural strength and way on the narrow path leading to eternity with Him.

Holy Living

I beseech you therefore, brethren, by the mercies of God, that ye present your bodies a living sacrifice, holy, acceptable unto God, which is your reasonable service. (Romans 12:1 KJV)

This verse contains an imperative, imploring or commanding statement calling for holy living. It calls for us to live a sanctified and set apart life acceptable according to god's holy standards. God is beseeching, or begging, His spiritual children to live sacrificially unto Him, not unto man and the standards of the world.

For God hath not called us unto uncleanness, but unto holiness. (1 Thessalonians 4:7 KJV)

God has set commandments and principles forth for us in His Word. These are quite the opposite of man's shallow and selfishness based and established upon the shifting sands of the world. Holiness is living separated unto Christ and apart from the world. Holiness and worldliness are contrasting, or heading in opposite directions. These paths are separate or dividing pathways. A person cannot have one foot walking towards God's holiness and the other foot walking along the path of the world towards the things of man.

Holiness affects our physical body. Holiness affects are thinking. Holiness is living in a state of ever increasing spirituality. Living in holiness means our spiritual essence or our soul and our physical bodies are made alive unto Christ and becoming spiritually deadened to the ways, thoughts, lifestyle, and mannerisms of this world. Holiness is living in subjection to Christ.

This holiness in one's life does not mean sinless living, for that is impossible on this side of heaven. Holy living while we are amid the sinful inclination of man here on earth is only possible when one lives spiritually through Jesus Christ, but for the grace of God go YOU and I and anyone who has Jesus Christ spiritually alive or quickened in their heart.

If we say that we have no sin, we deceive ourselves, and the truth is not in us. (1 John 1:8 KJV)

Does a person just wake up one morning and providentially receive the capability to live in holiness and subjection to Christ? No, quickening from the Holy Spirit does come upon a person when they place faith;

even as small as mustard seed, in Jesus Christ. However holy living unto Christ is a process of a lifetime on earth.

There is positional sanctification and personal sanctification. Positional sanctification is that "swoosh moment" when the Holy Spirit quickens the dead spirit in the heart of a person to be spiritually alive. Personal sanctification is a daily walk with God as we live on earth. It is walking with God on a path towards eternity and forsaking the god of this earth. It is feeding our spiritual nature and forsaking our sinful nature. It is that spiritual boxing match that Paul faced in Romans chapter seven when he said:

For the good that I would I do not: but the evil which I would not, that I do. Now if I do that I would not, it is no more I that do it, but sin that dwelleth in me. I find then a law, that, when I would do good, evil is present with me. For I delight in the law of God after the inward man (Romans 7:19-22 KJV)

Living holy for Jesus Christ while on this earth is being spiritually positioned in God's army. God's army is the only army ever to have the victory in hand before the battles are over because we serve a Savior who's risen and alive. This membership in God's holy army "marks" each person as living in opposition to the god of this world. Holy living is marching forward in His army towards eternity.

His army is always protected with His armor and uses His Word as a sharp, cutting spiritual sword to combat heartily in hand to hand battles; giving God all the glory and honor for the victory. The Bible contains all the holy training and weaponry necessary to march towards eternity in His army.

Living holy and peaceful lives in this sin saturated world does cause those around to sit up and take notice. True holy living separates one from the way the world lives, and outwardly shines glory for Jesus Christ. Without God's army persistently putting on their armor and marching forward through sin and trials and storms of life, living peaceable and contented lives full of joy so others can observe this steadfastness and hope as they wait for eternity. Without living holy and pursuing right relationships with others on earth man cannot please God and spend eternity in Heaven.

Follow peace with all men, and holiness, without which no man shall see the Lord. (Hebrews 12:14KJV)

Living holy will cause individuals to actively pursue purging sin out of their life, making a vessel unto honor for the glory of Jesus Christ. Holy living will purge anything that is ungodly or acting as leaven from their lives.

If a man therefore purge himself from these, he shall be a vessel unto honour, sanctified, and meet for the master's use, and prepared unto every good work. (2 Timothy 2:21 KJV)

This is a cleaning and bleaching process that takes time. It is not as easy as a shake or two of a "magic whitening wand" that instantly causes one's life to glitter and shine. Each individual who accepts Jesus Christ in faith will undertake this, sometimes grueling, but necessary scrubbing and bleaching process throughout life.

Sanctification entails picking up the cross and laying down all those sinful things hindering their walk with Him. A person cannot be prepared to march forward in an army headed to eternity in Heaven with the trappings of sin clinging like barnacles to their feet.

Wherefore seeing we also are compassed about with so great a cloud of witnesses, let us lay aside every weight, and the sin which doth so easily beset us, and let us run with patience the race that is set before us (Hebrews 12:1 KJV)

Throughout the entire bible God has called for holiness. In the Old Testament He made way for holiness through keeping of laws and the offering of sacrifices. This was not sufficient because it did not allow for the forgiveness of sin.

Speak unto all the congregation of the children of Israel, and say unto them, Ye shall be holy: for I the LORD your God am holy. (Leviticus 19:2 KJV)

In the New Testament God continues His call for holiness through His Son, Jesus Christ dying on the cross as a sacrifice for the forgiveness of sin. God himself has never changed. He has always been holy for He changes not. He gives us the grace needed to fulfill His will for our life.

Jesus Christ the same yesterday, and to day, and for ever. (Hebrews 13:8 KJV)

This grace He gives us enables us to live a life rich and full of His grace because Christ took away the penalty or wage for sins we have already committed, or will commit in the future. He has already preserved us blameless. He views us as without spot, or as white as snow, even as we sojourn here on earth and the sin nature ever before us as we march onwards towards eternity in Heaven.

And the very God of peace sanctify you wholly; and I pray God your whole spirit and soul and body be preserved blameless unto the coming of our Lord Jesus Christ. (1 Thessalonians 5:23 KJV)

FOR FURTHER CONTEMPLATION:

God's holiness should affect every aspect of our life upon this earth made complete in the Heavenly realm.

Sealed by the Holy Spirit

He has sealed His own spiritual family until the day of His eminent return to the earth. He guarantees eternal salvation for those who have professed by mouth and placed their faith in Him. We are sealed and no sin, whether it be by omission or commission, will serve to remove this eternal seal from our life. Nothing that any other person does can remove this seal from our lives. We are secure in His promises of eternal life and eternal blessings and joy to come.

In whom ye also trusted, after that ye heard the word of truth, the gospel of your salvation: in whom also after that ye believed, ye were sealed with that holy Spirit of promise   (Ephesians 1:13 KJV)

In the Roman world a seal was of great importance and nobody would lightly seek to tamper with or destroy a seal. Doing so would be to meddle in the affairs of the Roman government and call upon themselves sure and quick remedial action and likely death. The seal of God carries the ultimate weight of destruction and the wages of death to those who choose not to seek His holiness and will but choose to follow the god of this world suppressing the truth of God.

But to those who do seek His holiness:

And every man that hath this hope in him purifieth himself, even as he is pure. (1 John 3:3 KJV)

Lastly, this verse says every man that has hope of eternity purifies himself just as God is pure and holy. What a tremendous promise for us today. Faith in Jesus Christ feeds and fulfills our hope in an eternal life with Jesus Christ which nothing or anyone can take away.

FOR FURTHER CONTEMPLATION:

We are safe and secure this side of eternity by placing our faith in Him following His will for our lives purges sin out of our lives and makes us holy and Christ-like as we march onwards towards eternity. Entering into eternity with Him will complete our journey to holiness, Christlikeness and spiritual wholeness.

Righteous Judgment According to God's Word

Judge not according to the appearance, but judge righteous judgment. (John 7:24 KJV)

This verse from the book of John clearly indicates there is such a thing as righteous judgment. Often we hear remarks made such as "judge not lest you be judged, or "take the own mote out of your eye first." These remarks come from good well-meaning individuals who are loosely quoting scripture often out of biblical context, not always regarding proper circumstances and intent Jesus had for judging with righteous judgment.

Righteous judgment does not take into account appearance or assumed motives but relies solely upon the standard and truth of God's Holy Scriptures. Paul ascertains in the letter to the Thessalonians that as Christians we are, using God's measurement, to prove that which is true and upright. This proving magnifies those things or situations that are not holy in God's sight. This clear distinction allows us to turn away from those people and things surrounding us which are judged unrighteous in God's eyes, not our eyes, and turn toward that which is proven holy. This proving requires discernment and judgment and does not rely upon the opinion of man.

Prove all things; hold fast that which is good. (1 Thessalonians 5:21 KJV)

This righteous judgment is laid upon all things. The starting point for any judging is within oneself first. No man is qualified or called by God to look upon the interests and dealings of another individual unless his own house is in biblical order first and in conjunction with the walls of self-control surrounding him solidly in place as well. Putting his dwelling in order first removes any mote in his own eye, perfecting and clearing his vision about himself. It is looking in the mirror and digesting our own reflection against the holiness of a righteous God, contrasting unrighteousness. Doing this self-reflection will cause warts, moles, freckles leprous lesions and any hidden sins on the inside, to burst clearly noticeable to others and likely to ourselves as well in God's perfect timing.

Sometimes our overwhelming sin lurks about in our midst so slyly that we alone cannot discern it from our vantage point. Loving brothers or sisters need to step up and shine the light of His Word for us to see our situation more clearly without adding any contention or strife among brethren.

But he that is spiritual judgeth all things, yet he himself is judged of no man. (1 Corinthians 2:15 KJV)

If each person who professes Christ as the Lord of their life would take into account their own spiritual health and pulse, studying and praying steadfastly for holy maintenance and repairs needed in their own circumstances, there would be more spiritually sound, strong, Joyful, humble Christians walking in contrast to the darkness in our midst and less finger-pointing towards others around us.

Unrighteous judgment of others God condemns. This kind of judgment is hastily pointing fingers in prideful criticism and reproach, and daunting spiritual attacks; serving no purpose other than to dishearten others and giving no glory to God.

Judge not, that ye be not judged For with what judgment ye judge, ye shall be judged: and with what measure ye mete, it shall be measured to you again. And why beholdest thou the mote that is in thy brother's eye, but considerest not the beam that is in thine own eye? Or how wilt thou say to thy brother, Let me pull out the mote out of thine eye; and, behold, a beam is in thine own eye? Thou hypocrite, first cast out the beam out of thine own eye; and then shalt thou see clearly to cast out the mote out of thy brother's eye. (Matthew 7:1-5 KJV)

This is not a command forbidding judgment of another but against wrongful judgment of others. Every believer has a duty, out of love, to consider the fruits of others who are in their spiritual family, especially those who are teaching others. The Bible tells us we can know others by their fruits or by their lack of fruit thereof. It is wrong, however, to come to pointed conclusions about another individual through man's imperfect reasoning. The righteous judgment and spiritual approach God modeled throughput scripture is necessary in approaching a brother or sister who needs reproach according to the standards God has set forth. God's righteous judgment is based upon His love and perfect holiness.

Beware of false prophets, which come to you in sheep's clothing, but inwardly they are ravening wolves. Ye shall know them by their fruits. Do men gather grapes of thorns, or figs of thistles? Even so every good tree bringeth forth good fruit; but a corrupt tree bringeth forth evil fruit. A good tree cannot bring forth evil fruit, neither can a corrupt tree bring forth good fruit. Every tree that bringeth not forth good fruit is hewn down, and cast into the fire. Wherefore by their fruits ye shall know them. (Matthew 7:15-20 KJV)

And he spake this parable unto certain which trusted in themselves that they were righteous, and despised others: Two men went up into the temple to pray; the one a Pharisee, and the other a publican. The Pharisee stood and prayed thus with himself, God, I thank thee, that I am not as other men are, extortioners, unjust, adulterers, or even as this publican. I fast twice in the week, I give tithes of all that I possess. And the publican, standing afar off, would not lift up so much as his eyes unto heaven, but smote upon his breast, saying, God be merciful to me a sinner. I tell you, this man went down to his house justified rather than the other: for every one that exalteth himself shall be abased; and he that humbleth himself shall be exalted. (Luke 18:9-14 KJV)

We cannot judge the heart or motives of another individual only by their outward actions and fruit, or lack thereof. Jesus looks straight through all the outer paraphernalia and adornment and cuts straight to the heart of the issue, a spiritual chink or fissure of the heart.

FOR FURTHER CONTEMPLATION:

Those who profess to be Christians must always remember the pit from which we were lifted. How we dug and clawed at the sides of the pit trying to crawl out of the deep black hole upon our own merits and weakness- unable to lift our own selves out of the miry mess but for the powerful hand of God which did lift us out of the dreadful pit of sin.

Loose Him and Let Him Go

And he that was dead came forth, bound hand and foot with graveclothes: and his face was bound about with a napkin. Jesus saith unto them, Loose him, and let him go. (John 11:44 KJV)

Remember Lazarus who was bound and stinking horrendously after being dead already four days? Jesus loosed him and let him go but the odor lingered about Him.

Christians today must help remove any stinking clothes from our fellow brothers and sisters who are new-born babes in Christ. Therefore, test, examine, discern and Judge between good and evil according to His scripture and the spiritual strength and discernment Christ has given us; helping to remove those soiled clothes from others who are gaining their new found spiritual legs.

But strong meat belongeth to them that are of full age, even those who by reason of use have their senses exercised to discern both good and evil. (Hebrews 5:14 KJV)

FOR FURTHER CONTEMPLATION:

Do you or others in your midst still have the cloths of death wrapped tightly around you?

Loving AND Judging Others

Ye judge after the flesh; I judge no man. (John 8:15 KJV)

Judge others not according to our quickly stirred up emotions, feelings, fleshly passions or in anger, coming to a hasty assumption without sufficient facts or information to form a solid conclusion. The hidden things of a man only Christ can see and ascertain.

He that answereth a matter before he heareth it, it is folly and shame unto him. (Proverbs 18:13 KJV)

We must know the Word of God and have it buried within our heart to function Christ-like and spiritually in this world of darkness and evil deeds.

Study to shew thyself approved unto God, a workman that needeth not to be ashamed, rightly dividing the word of truth. (2 Timothy 2:15 KJV)

And we must understand how to utilize His Word as Christ intended bringing out His supernatural power as we sojourn here on earth:

For the word of God is quick, and powerful, and sharper than any twoedged sword, piercing even to the dividing asunder of soul and spirit, and of the joints and marrow, and is a discerner of the thoughts and intents of the heart. (Hebrews 4:12 KJV)

All scripture is given by inspiration of God, and is profitable for doctrine, for reproof, for correction, for instruction in righteousness: (2 Timothy 3:16 KJV)

These were more noble than those in Thessalonica, in that they received the word with all readiness of mind, and searched the scriptures daily, whether those things were so. (Acts 17:11 KJV)

Therefore thou art inexcusable, O man, whosoever thou art that judgest: for wherein thou judgest another, thou condemnest thyself; for thou that judgest doest the same things. But we are sure that the judgment of God is according to truth against them which commit such things. (Romans 2:1-2 KJV)

YOU are a walking advertisement speaking for and against the Lord by your actions; or inaction. We must be spirit controlled. Christ like. There is true spiritual minded wisdom that naturally comes outward from our desire to be Christ-like.

And this I pray, that your love may abound yet more and more in knowledge and in all judgment; That ye may approve things that are excellent; that ye may be sincere and without offence till the day of Christ; Being filled with the fruits of righteousness, which are by Jesus Christ, unto the glory and praise of God. (Philippians 1:9-11 KJV)

Passion for God's Word must be tempered by and guided by Love. This is the responsibility of the children of God. We are called to be ye separate or not walk along with those who are living worldly to do so we must make a judgment that is set apart from those that live in the world and any who might compromise or weaken God's Word.

There are different forms of judgment in the world today. Judgments against immorality, truth verses error, holy living verses unholy living, but only one true standard or measurement which is the Word of God.

FOR FURTHER CONTEMPLATION:

What basis do you use in formulating opinions and judgment of others? Your own merits or founded upon the holiness of God and His Word?

A Financial Song and Dance

Can you point to any verses indicating the Lord's work was ever maintained or sustained through acquiring debt in scripture? A church loaded with debt is not necessarily provision from God or answers to prayers of a well-intentioned congregation bent on being benevolent.

A financial song and dance routine is trending in countless churches today. Many congregations are struggling in the financial arena. Offering plates are coming back from the aisles often lighter as some professing Christians are bringing in less tithes and offerings into the storehouse.

Will a man rob God? Yet ye have robbed me. But ye say, Wherein have we robbed thee? In tithes and offerings. Ye are cursed with a curse: for ye have robbed me, even this whole nation. Bring ye all the tithes into the storehouse, that there may be meat in mine house, and prove me now herewith, saith the LORD of hosts, if I will not open you the windows of heaven, and pour you out a blessing, that there shall not be room enough to receive it. (Malachi 3:8-10 KJV)

There is much false teaching flourishing among Bible believing Christians concerning money in today's church. Some teachers may proclaim tithing was under the old covenant in the Old Testament; therefore man is no longer bound to tithe in the New Testament church today. This is false doctrine as tithing was established in the Old Testament prior to Moses receiving the Law from God; therefore tithing is not bound together with following the law of the Old Covenant.

And Melchizedek king of Salem brought forth bread and wine: and he was the priest of the most high God. And he blessed him, and said, Blessed be Abram of the most high God, possessor of heaven and earth: And blessed be the most high God, which hath delivered thine enemies into thy hand. And he gave him tithes of all. (Genesis 14:18-20KJV)

One looming factor affecting church finances is the doors of many churches revolve continually bringing people in and out of attendance. Tithes and offerings can fluctuate like the wind, ultimately making any kind of financial planning akin to taking a stab in the dark or blindly pulling figures out of midair when budgeting. These parameters do not necessarily form a consistent and reliable blueprint for church leaders to plan for the future.

Sometimes leaders push congregations to rely heavily upon future expectations and offerings as the members are led to vote for their church to assume a debt for a church build or expansion plan. The project may seem financially sound today but those same members and/or church leaders may leave the church tomorrow and not be personally responsible for any lingering or prolonged debt. Future repayment is pushed onto a faithful remnant and those joining the church in the future.

If every church member were held personally responsible for repayment; diving head first into a building project might be harder to initiate. Church membership might approach a building project by relying more upon the Lord's leading by much prayer and contemplation, not following man's ideas and taking a leap in the dark.

God instructs us both personally as individuals and collectively about financial affairs in His Word. We are to be a light shining brightly in the darkness, including in the realm of worldly financial affairs, willing to teach and mirror holy financial responsibility. Proper fiscal responsibility may not always include taking on more debt. Christians are to give, via freewill offering, to the Lord's work through their tithes and offerings. Some give out of any portion leftover after everything else is paid, others by following the law grudgingly, and others give sacrificially and generously beyond ten percent.

Every man according as he purposeth in his heart, so let him give; not grudgingly, or of necessity: for God loveth a cheerful giver. And God is able to make all grace abound toward you; that ye, always having all sufficiency in all things, may abound to every good work (2 Corinthians 9:7-8 KJV)

If a church seeks funding from the worldly banking system to finance a building project for buildings needed to worship and teach the truth of God's Word, is that contradicting the His nature and holiness who could, if it is in His will, provide any necessary money by divine providence?

Remember the manna the Lord provided for the Israelites as they roamed about in the desert, fulfilling their needs quite sufficiently and consistently for forty years. We are called to be a peculiar people separating ourselves from the values and the "standard operating procedures" the world upholds. This must also include being separated in the financial and business arena and include how churches conduct their financial affairs in this world. God would not lead a church into supporting a mission field or spiritual undertaking without providing the needed financial structure and support.

Nobody can ever out give the giving of God. The opposite of borrowing funds is giving money away. God wants to bless His people and churches to overflowing.

Give, and it shall be given unto you; good measure, pressed down, and shaken together, and running over, shall men give into your bosom. For with the same measure that ye mete withal it shall be measured to you again. (Luke 6:38 KJV))

Maybe the problem lies in the fact that many individuals and churches are not always obedient to God's commandments. Many are harboring sin personally, and in their church. This can place roadblocks in the path of the growth, for getting the gospel out, and spiritual growth of its members.

The rich ruleth over the poor, and the borrower is servant to the lender. (Proverbs 22:7 KJV)

If we look into the Old Testament research the matter of debt, the bible teaches that the borrower becomes a slave to the lender. Looking at debt from this viewpoint, burdening the church with debt is totally contrary to the gospel. The gospel is all about freedom and breaking away from bondage and oppression and sin. Not all debt is considered bondage; however, excessive debt certainly would be akin to a yoke of bondage encircling and suppressing the functioning of the church and it membership.

In the New Testament the Apostle Paul wrote to the Galatians:

Stand fast therefore in the liberty wherewith Christ hath made us free, and be not entangled again with the yoke of bondage. (Galatians 5:1 KJV)

Anyone who preaches a "gospel" which includes an excessive debt burden, and proclaiming it to be God's will to do His work through acquiring debt, does he preach a false and misleading gospel message? Debt is not freedom; it is bondage! Promoting bondage in the church is a matter which must be closely examined in the light of His Word and entered into carefully and after much careful prayer and study. Debt can be necessary at times, even in a church, but not always the most beneficial avenue or the path God would lead a congregation or an individual in Christ down in all given circumstances.

When a church goes into debt are they serving two masters? The danger of compromising the truth becomes very real. One cannot be loyal to Christ and at the same time not be loyal to the truth, because Jesus says, "I am the truth." A church in debt can easily become a church of divided loyalties. The church and it's leadership may have the best and honest intentions of staying absolutely loyal to the truth, but in times of financial trouble looming; in meeting financial obligations they may opt to do all, or anything necessary to please the people, so they, in turn, will continue to attend the church services giving loyally and sacrificially their tithes and offerings.

God tells us to walk by faith; Money conditions us to walk by sight.

For we walk by faith, not by sight: (2 Corinthians 5:7 KJV)

God tells us to set our minds on the things above; Money, or lack thereof, tends to draw our attention to things of the earth; the possessions we have or those we might think we have need of.

Behold the fowls of the air: for they sow not, neither do they reap, nor gather into barns; yet your heavenly Father feedeth them. Are ye not much better than they? Which of you by taking thought can add one cubit unto his stature? And why take ye thought for raiment? Consider the lilies of the field, how they grow; they toil not, neither do they spin": And yet I say unto you, That even Solomon in all his glory was not arrayed like one of these. (Matthew 6:26-29 KJV)

God tells us not to be anxious for anything; to keep our focus on Him. The truth is that the church cannot serve both God and Money and remain unified. Countless churches have been set back spiritually by an inability to sustain or pay off debt. This can create an oppressive and burdensome atmosphere where hope is pressed down and false doctrine can thrive and flourish. Essentially God may even be standing outside many churches that are sinking fast knee-deep in debt and looking in forlornly at their lukewarm disorder. He has promptly been ushered to the curb and rejected so a weaker message of compromise and half-truths can be given from the pulpit to sustain their current membership numbers.

Jesus told us to spread the Gospel. He gave us all the great commission as our life long mission for serving the Lord and spreading forth the gospel. Fulfilling this great commission takes us out of our church house and onto the highways and byways of life to find those He leads us to who need to hear the message of the gospel of Christ. People do not come knocking on massive and fancily built church doors begging to hear the message of salvation.

Frankly, our service to Christ most often takes place outside the church house. Men tend to place their focus, attention, and service inside the church house. We must get ourselves busy in God's back yard, in our immediate area, and across the oceans; the harvest of souls is ripe for our witnessing. Where God leads He also provides the means to accomplish His will.

From Genesis to revelation God is known as many names that all individually encompassed the nature of God. One of these names is "Jehova-Jireh" or God will provide. Not did provide, but will provide in the present tense. He will provide for His own children now and for future needs. He continually provides from Genesis in the past all the way up to Revelation in the future.

And Abraham lifted up his eyes, and looked, and behold behind him a ram caught in a thicket by his horns: and Abraham went and took the ram, and offered him up for a burnt offering in the stead of his son. And Abraham called the name of that place Jehovahjireh: as it is said to this day, In the mount of the LORD it shall be seen. (Genesis 22:13-14 KJV)

One of the most important things to take note of in these verses is that God did provide a ram as a substitute sacrifice for Abraham instead of the need to sacrifice his own son, as Abraham was obedient to God. Abraham's obedience was necessary to fulfill the will of God. This was a picture of Jesus's death on the cross for our sins. Jesus's obedience to the cross was necessary to fulfill God's will. God looks for our obedience to His will in our life as well.

For which of you, intending to build a tower, sitteth not down first, and counteth the cost, whether he have sufficient to finish it? Lest haply, after he hath laid the foundation, and is not able to finish it, all that behold it begin to mock him, Saying, This man began to build, and was not able to finish. (Luke 14:28-30 KJV)

Faith is a huge contributing factor in planning church finances but it is not the only dynamic in the decision-making process. Your local bank's accounting depends on actual dollars deposited and not on a faith basis of collecting funds. Therefore, faith plays a big role in trusting God for the necessary resources, but does not account for the entire financial well-being of a church. Financial faith then is not simply testing God to meet the perceived needs of the church, but faith requires obedience to God along with discernment and planning carefully for the future according to sound scriptural doctrine, avoiding any appearance of wrong mismanagement, and accountability to others.

Any church project has two types of costs; cost of materials from start to finish of the project, and the all-important personal cost of obedience to Christ in the center of the project at hand.

In conclusion: God wants to bless His church. God wants to bless His people. He wants to provide for His will to be done. God wants all churches to be abounding in His work. He is ready to bless those churches who give Him first place, who give sacrificially over and above what He asks. He does not need His ten percent back entrusted to you; but in obedience to Him and His will he takes note of those who continue moving the circle of blessing, bringing back to His storehouse that which He gave, keeping this circle of blessing moving towards others in need.

Give, and it shall be given unto you; good measure, pressed down, and shaken together, and running over, shall men give into your bosom. For with the same measure that ye mete withal it shall be measured to you again. (Luke 6:38 KJV)

But my God shall supply all your need according to his riches in glory by Christ Jesus. (Philippians 4:19 KJV)

FOR FURTHER CONTEMPLATION:

God wants to meet your personal needs. God wants to meet the needs of His church. God abundantly supplies all needs to those who walk in obedience to Him. Are you searching the scriptures and meeting with Him in your prayer closet to hear His will for your life?

Who Is Responsible for Jesus's Death?

And when they were come to the place, which is called Calvary, there they crucified him, and the malefactors, one on the right hand, and the other on the left. (Luke 23:33KJV)

"There they crucified him." Who? You say, "The Jews did it." This charge has been laid to the Jews for years. They have been referred to as the Christ-crucifiers, as the God-murderers, and because of this they have been persecuted as the ones who crucified our Saviour.

To be sure, the Jews must take their part of the blame for His death. It was the Jews who laid hold upon Him in the Garden of Gethsemane. Jesus Christ stood before Annas and Caiaphas, their high priests. He was tried by the Sanhedrin. His own people, the Jews, called Him a blasphemer worthy of death. It was the Jews who cried out, "Crucify him, Crucify him." It was the Jews who took counsel against Him to put Him to death. So the Jews must share their part in the responsibility for the death of Jesus Christ on the cross. "There they crucified him." Who? The Jews.

However it was the Romans, not the Jews, who actually killed Him. So the Romans must take their part of the blame for the crucifixion of Jesus. The Jews didn't have the power to put anyone to death. The Jews were under Roman rule and could only try a man and declare him worthy of death; but the final decision was with the power of Rome. The power of capital punishment was not committed to the Jews but only to the hands of the Romans. When Jesus came before the Sanhedrin, they found Him worthy of death; but they had to go to Pilate, the Roman governor, in order to get the death penalty. Pilate said to Jesus in **John 19:10 ". . . I have power to crucify thee, and have power to release thee," or, "to let thee go."** Pilate wasn't just bluffing; nor was he simply trying to frighten Jesus when he said, "I have power to crucify thee," or "I have the power to release thee." He did have that power. As the Roman governor, that authority was in his hands. He could say, "Let Him go," and the soldiers would release Him. So the authority to put Jesus to death was in the hands of the Roman governor.

Pilate turned Him over to the Roman soldiers. Who scourged Jesus? The Romans. Who spit in Jesus' face until the spittle ran down His beard? The Romans. Who put the purple robe on His back? The Romans. Who placed the reed in the hand of Jesus? The Romans. Who bowed and mocked Jesus Christ and said, "Hail king of the Jews!" The Romans. Who laid the two hundred-pound cross upon the back of Jesus and compelled Him to carry it a bloody mile? The Romans. Who laid Jesus down upon that cross and drove the nails through His hands and feet? It was the Romans. Who divided His clothing among them? The Romans. Who sat at the foot of the cross and gambled for His cloak that was woven without seam? The Romans. Who put the inscription over the cross, "Jesus of Nazareth the King of the Jews"? It was the Romans. Why do I say it was the Romans? Because the Jews went to the Romans and begged them to change the inscription. "Write not, The King of the Jews; but that he said, I am King of the Jews." The Jews did not want to recognize Jesus Christ as their king, so requested the Roman government to change the inscription. Pilate answered, "What I have written I have written."

Who sealed the tomb in which Jesus was laid? The Romans, Who stood guard around that tomb daring the world to molest it? It was the Romans. So the Jews are not alone in their blame, guilt and crucifixion of Jesus. The Romans, the Gentiles, are also responsible. But I believe if the Romans had not given authority for Jesus Christ to be crucified, the Jews would have taken Him into their own hands and crucified Hi, they like they later killed Stephen.

On the other hand, I believe if the Jews had not tried Jesus because of His claim to the Messiahship, the Romans would have taken Jesus Christ and crucified Him without the Jews, as they later did James and Paul. Both Jews and Gentiles are guilty of His crucifixion. "There they crucified him."

The Jews – yes. The Romans – yes. And you and I. In the final analysis, it was your sin and my sin that nailed Jesus Christ to the cross. We are as much responsible for the death of Jesus as the Jews who cried, "Crucify him, Crucify him!" As responsible for the death of Jesus as the Romans, who drove the nails through His hands and feet. It was our hand on the hammer that drove the nails because our sin nailed Christ to the cross.

A man once dreamed that he was witnessing the scourging of Jesus. In his dream he screamed, "Stop it! Stop it! Stop it!" When the Roman soldier with the scourge in his hand looked around, the man saw his own face!

If you close your eyes and visualize the Roman soldier scourging Jesus Christ until His inner organs lie at His feet in a pool of blood, and if your imagination is as vivid as mine, you can see yourself with a scourge in your own hand laying the stripes on the back of the Son of God.

"There they crucified him." Who? You and me. We were there! "There they crucified him." We did it! Our sin did it! Those still without the Saviour are still in the throng.

Jesus did this for you and I. He chose to suffer this humiliation that we may come to Him and have eternal life.

FOR FURTHER CONTEMPLATION:

Jesus paid it all. All to Him I owe. Jesus paid it all. All to Him I owe.

Are You Living to Die?

There was a certain rich man, which was clothed in purple and fine linen, and fared sumptuously every day: And there was a certain beggar named Lazarus, which was laid at his gate, full of sores, And desiring to be fed with the crumbs which fell from the rich man's table: moreover the dogs came and licked his sores. And it came to pass, that the beggar died, and was carried by the angels into Abraham's bosom: the rich man also died, and was buried; And in hell he lift up his eyes, being in torments, and seeth Abraham afar off, and Lazarus in his bosom. (Luke 16:19-23 KJV)

The rich man in Luke 16 died unprepared. I am sure many thought he was well prepared. No doubt he had provided well for his family we read in **Luke 16:19 There was a certain rich man, which was clothed in purple and fine linen, and fared sumptuously every day.** He no doubt had a good bank account. Probably he had a good insurance policy. Had anything happened to him no doubt his family would have been better off financially, as it is in the case of most of us. He had made preparations to live; but he had not made preparations to die.

He was like the rich farmer who had been blessed of God. His crops brought forth so plentifully that he had no place to bestow his goods. He said to himself, where shall I put all my goods? I know what I'll do; I'll tear down my old barns and build new ones. Then I'll say, Soul, thou hast much goods laid up in store. Take thine ease, eat, drink and be merry. He made preparations to live; but he made no preparations to die.

When you die, nobody is going to ask, who your father was, or how much money you had in the bank, or whether you owned your own business or worked for someone else. When you die, nobody is going to ask where you went to college.

When we depart this world the only thing that will matter is: Are you spiritually dead or alive? Do you know Jesus Christ as your Saviour? Have you been born again?

A very wealthy man had died. After the funeral service a little boy was riding in a wagon with an old man. The man was talking about how much money the deceased had. He must have been worth several hundred thousand dollars. Finally he said, "I wonder how much he left." The little fellow replied, "He left it all." When you die, you leave it all. You can't carry one dime with you.

The rich man died unprepared, **"was buried; And in Hell he lift up his eyes, being in torments." It says that the beggar died, "and was carried by the angels into Abraham's bosom."**

The beggar died. They dragged his body off the street, threw it in the cart and wheeled it away. He had no funeral, no flowers, no singing – nothing. But he was carried by angels to Abraham's bosom. He died prepared, while the rich man died unprepared. The beggar didn't go to Heaven because he was poor, and the rich man didn't go to Hell because he was rich. The rich man went to Hell because he rejected Jesus, and the poor beggar went to Heaven because he accepted Christ and was born again.

FOR FURTHER CONTEMPLATION:

Don't die unprepared. Trust Jesus Christ as your personal Saviour.

Is there life after death?

Here are three different earthly perspectives of this question: is there life after death?

The first come from the materialist. His reply is a quick and short, "No." The materialist claims that the sum total of man is flesh, bone and blood. Ask the materialist, "Where does one go when he dies?" and he will answer, "Nowhere. Earth to earth: ashes to ashes, and dust to dust; (which in the Bible they will gladly point out for you.) The soul is a function of the brain they will say."

Someone once said, "Knock me on the head; where then is my soul?"

The second answer comes from the **scientist**: but when it comes to the question, "If a man die, shall he live again?" The scientist's lips are sealed. He has no answer. Science is organized knowledge; and this knowledge is of things seen and does not include anything not able to be physically seen.

But the Bible says in *2 Corinthians 4:18 ". . . the things which are seen are temporal; but the things which are not seen are eternal."*

The scientist has no scientific way of proving life after death, since there is no way to test and experiment in the spiritual arena. The scientist can deal only with those things he can taste, touch, hear, see, and smell all things having to do with our five God given senses. So when a scientist tells me where I came from or where I'm going, he's completely out of his working and familiar field which is from this world.

The third answer comes from the **agnostic**. A word invented by this world. It is a transformation or worldly alteration of a Greek based word which means "unknown." The agnostic does not say for sure that there is not life after death; simply that we cannot know." He is right that if man leaves out the equation of divine knowledge contained in the Word of God man cannot know for sure of an eternal realm. It would be trying to look at things spiritually with a dead spiritual heart. Spiritual things cannot be discerned living in spiritual death.

What was our Lord's answer to the question is there life after death in the Bible?

"If a man die, shall he live again? Jesus answered that question in *John 11:25-26 KJV "Jesus said unto her, I am the resurrection, and the life: he that believeth in me,* *though he were dead, yet shall he live: And whosoever liveth and believeth in me shall never die."*

He answered it again when He said to His disciples in *(John 14:1-3 KJV) "Let not your heart be troubled: ye believe in God, believe also in me. In my Father's house are many mansions: if it were not so, I would have told you. I go to prepare a place for you. And if I go and prepare a place for you, I will come again, and receive you unto myself; that where I am, there ye may be also."*

Our Lord was about to be separated from His disciples by death but He assured them that they would meet again. **"I will . . . receive you unto myself" teaches reunion; "myself"** teaches recognition in the life to come. How would the disciples know that they had been received unto the Lord unless they recognized Him?

FOR FURTHER CONTEMPLATION:

Do you know for sure will you live in the eternal realm for all eternity? The answer is definitive in the Bible: with God in eternal life or without Him in the fires of Hell.

Is Heaven a real place?

(lJohn 14:2-3 KJV) Jesus said "In my Father's house are many mansions: if it were not so, I would have told you. I go to prepare a place for you. And if I go and prepare a place for you, I will come again, and receive you unto myself; that where I am, there ye may be also."

Here our Lord calls Heaven a place.

(Matthew 6:19-20 KJV) exhorts, "Lay not up for yourselves treasures upon earth, where moth and rust doth corrupt, and where thieves break through and steal: But lay up for yourselves treasures in heaven, where neither moth nor rust doth corrupt, and where thieves do not break through nor steal."

This could only be said of a real, literal, physical place. Some think Heaven is a state of mind; but moth and rust cannot corrupt the state of mind; thieves cannot break into a state of mind. That could only be said of a real, literal, physical place.

Revelation 21:15 gives the measurement of the Holy City. If you multiplied the cubits into feet, then divided the feet into miles, you would discover that the Holy City is 1,500 miles square. This could not be said of a state of mine. It could only be said of a real, literal place.

FOR FURTHER CONTEMPLATION:

Do you know if you are going to Heaven? If you don't please don't let another day go by without making sure! The Bible says you can know for sure if you are going to Heaven in **1st John 5:13**

Spiritual Dry Bones

The hand of the LORD was upon me, and carried me out in the spirit of the LORD, and set me down in the midst of the valley which was full of bones, And caused me to pass by them round about: and, behold, there were very many in the open valley; and, lo, they were very dry. And he said unto me, Son of man, can these bones live? And I answered, O Lord GOD, thou knowest. Again he said unto me, Prophesy upon these bones, and say unto them, O ye dry bones, hear the word of the LORD. Thus saith the Lord GOD unto these bones; Behold, I will cause breath to enter into you, and ye shall live: And I will lay sinews upon you, and will bring up flesh upon you, and cover you with skin, and put breath in you, and ye shall live; and ye shall know that I am the LORD. So I prophesied as I was commanded: and as I prophesied, there was a noise, and behold a shaking, and the bones came together, bone to his bone. And when I beheld, lo, the sinews and the flesh came up upon them, and the skin covered them above: but there was no breath in them. Then said he unto me, Prophesy unto the wind, prophesy, son of man, and say to the wind, Thus saith the Lord GOD; Come from the four winds, O breath, and breathe upon these slain, that they may live. So I prophesied as he commanded me, and the breath came into them, and they lived, and stood up upon their feet, an exceeding great army. Then he said unto me, Son of man, these bones are the whole house of Israel: behold, they say, Our bones are dried, and our hope is lost: we are cut off for our parts. Therefore prophesy and say unto them, Thus saith the Lord GOD; Behold, O my people, I will open your graves, and cause you to come up out of your graves, and bring you into the land of Israel. And ye shall know that I am the LORD, when I have opened your graves, O my people, and brought you up out of your graves, And shall put my spirit in you, and ye shall live, and I shall place you in your own land: then shall ye know that I the LORD have spoken it, and performed it, saith the LORD. (Ezekiel 37:1-14 KJV)

Many biblical scholars believe The Valley of dry Bones is an allegory or a prophetic vision of the future and not an actual reference to a place. It is at the very least an illustration concerning the Jewish people and the entire nation of Israel. The dry bones are a depiction their spiritual deprivation and their future restoration prophetically mentioned throughout scripture.

The Jewish people's spiritual restoration is likened to a reconstruction of a physical human body. These Biblical passages describe, piece by piece, this restoration process, even down to the ligaments and sinews connecting bones together with flesh to cover them above this inner handiwork.

This allegory or Old Testament Parable is a picture of, foremost, the salvation and restoration of Jewish people prophesied yet to come in the end times. Secondly, this paints a picture in of New Testament times of the salvation process of human souls, whosoever shall believe, in Jesus Christ by faith.

The apostle Paul, the apostle God called to witness specifically to the Gentile people, was himself knocked down in fright and greatly humbled as he came face to face with his own "dry bones existence" traveling along the Damascus Road.

Paul's weary and wicked existence, in extreme opposition to God, was straightway transformed and filled into a spiritual filled presence used to further His gospel. Paul's extraordinary salvation paints a wonderful picture; going from a heap of spiritual dry bones lying upon the roadway, with a wounded spirit who had bruised and battered God's own children, affectionately scooped up in the strong arms of a loving God and made of great use in the Holy plans of the lord for His glory.

Salvation is possible in a person who has come to the end of themselves seeing their need for the authority of god, lying prostrate, broken in spirit and in a heap of dry bones, in front of God's holy and illuminating presence. Often people are drawn, haggard, wasted from continuing to struggle and exist without any spiritual fuel energizing this meager existence. Literally they have wasted away to a broken existence like dry bones. Salvation is a lifesaving infusion of Calvary's blood injected into those bones. It is the presence forever more of the Holy Spirit, who brings fullness of joy which lasts forever more; overflowing into every aspect of one's life.

A merry heart doeth good like a medicine: but a broken spirit drieth the bones. (Proverbs 17:22KJV)

Those who have received this life-giving infusion of new life through faith in Jesus Christ are different than those who have chosen to live and serve the god of this world. Any person living in this new life with Christ should have a merry heart and joy unspeakable, a melody instilled within their heart on a continuous loop, not a somber, dry, dreary existence, without hope, as many unsaved persons living for the world often outwardly display. Without this inoculation of the Holy Spirit through salvation there is no hope found living in a futile existence in this world. There is no hope for the future without the heart knowledge of a promise of eternal life waiting in heaven.

A Christian, who has settled the matter of eternity, should be the most joyful, peaceful, exuberant, lively persons on this earth. Going to church, working or sharing space alongside or living with a Christian should not be a downcast, dreary, hopeless existence like many desperate and futile homeless living under a bridge or along a street, or attending a funeral of a friend or relative who never believed in Jesus Christ. Joy should be present in any circumstance a Christian finds himself in.

Everlasting joy is what many Jewish people, returning to their homeland in Israel, will find upon their hearts, as the Lord returns making their salvation complete.

And the ransomed of the LORD shall return, and come to Zion with songs and everlasting joy upon their heads: they shall obtain joy and gladness, and sorrow and sighing shall flee away. (Isaiah 35:10 KJV)

Just as the Jewish people will be filled with everlasting joy as they return unto their land of promise one day; those of us who have salvation in the Lord today should have that unspeakable and wonderful joy living inside our heart. Any affliction or towering wave of trials we come across can be an avenue filled with joy and eternal perseverance when walking alongside God.

If you, Christian, find yourself continually dreary and down in the dumps, becoming dry in the bones; you must ask yourself if you harboring sin and disobedience in your walk with Christ. The Christian life is meant to be filled with joy and supernaturally overflowing. Have you placed distance between yourself and God because of sin in your life?

If you are missing joy, a key ingredient of the Christian life, the place to start is within your own heart.

FOR FURTHER CONTEMPLATION:

Read **Psalm 51: 1-12** and consider how David poured His heart out to the Lord in repentance, confession, and sorrow over his sin. In verse twelve David then prays to have the joy of his salvation restored.

Is this the "holy remedy" for your present sad and sorrowful heart condition?

Restore unto me the joy of thy salvation; and uphold me with thy free spirit. (Psalms 51:12 KJV)

Is Your Manna Moldy?

Then said the LORD unto Moses, Behold, I will rain bread from heaven for you; and the people shall go out and gather a certain rate every day, that I may prove them, whether they will walk in my law, or no. And it shall come to pass, that on the sixth day they shall prepare that which they bring in; and it shall be twice as much as they gather daily." And Moses and Aaron said unto all the children of Israel, At even, then ye shall know that the LORD hath brought you out from the land of Egypt: And in the morning, then ye shall see the glory of the LORD; for that he heareth your murmurings against the LORD: and what are we, that ye murmur against us? And Moses said, This shall be, when the LORD shall give you in the evening flesh to eat, and in the morning bread to the full; for that the LORD heareth your murmurings which ye murmur against him: and what are we? your murmurings are not against us, but against the LORD. (Exodus 16:4-8 KJV)

The Israelite's were in the middle of the wilderness of the hot and harsh desert; marching out of Egypt and trudging towards the Promised Land. They soon began to realize their journey was not going to be easy or painless. In fact, it seemed to be downright horrible and relentless.

The Israelites began to feel miserable and to murmur and complain against Aaron and Moses because they felt lacked the necessary sustenance needed for their journey. They viewed their immediate circumstances, taking note of their lack of resources, removing their eyes off of God, who had already promised to divinely supply all their need.

God heard their complaining. God does not need a prosperous economy or bountiful fields full of harvest to provide for His children. He promised to provide an evening portion of quail; and manna every morning raining down with the dew from heaven for the Israelites.

God intended for the Israelites to gather this sustenance daily. Moses told them to gather just enough to cover their immediate needs, enough to provide for each man in their tent according to their eating. It was not necessary for them to gather and store these provisions towards future needs. His divine supply was promised to be new each morning, proving their faith in Him. The sixth day was an exception. God promised to provide twice as much on the fifth day, allowing them rest on the sixth day. They were bound under law from Moses to rest on this day, as God did rest after finishing His creation.

Some of the Israelites did not heed the words of Moses who told them not to leave the manna for the next morning. The manna which was kept left over for the next day now bred worms and stank. Harboring the manna angered Moses and each were told again to gather according to their immediate needs and the allowance made for the Sabbath day. The manna now left on the ground melted in the warmth of the sun each day. The Israelite's were fed this sustenance daily until they reached the Promised Land. This was forty years.

Today is your barn and silo filled to overflowing? Do you have more abundance than you can use for your immediate needs? God intends for us to be responsible in our stewardship of His resources; not expecting us to grip tightly all that he provides and Storing away treasures for rainy days or the needs of tomorrow. God is already at work in our tomorrows. He intends for us to keep the circle of blessing flowing towards others in need, especially those who are in the spiritual family of God.

When we pick up our cross living sold out to His will; God promises to supply our needs as we move in obedience to His call. Especially those who have honored Him faithfully; being good stewards of His time, service, and pleased Him with financial tithing as well.

But my God shall supply all your need according to his riches in glory by Christ Jesus. (Philippians 4:19 KJV)

Is your manna gathering mold, worms, rusting away, or lying in wait of corruption or thieves to confiscate and enjoy on their own selfish pleasures?

Lay not up for yourselves treasures upon earth, where moth and rust doth corrupt, and where thieves break through and steal: But lay up for yourselves treasures in heaven, where neither moth nor rust doth corrupt, and where thieves do not break through nor steal: For where your treasure is, there will your heart be also. (Matthew 6:19-21 KJV)

The world tells us to save for retirement, save for a rainy day, save for an economic disaster, save for a personal emergency and save, save, save.

Provision, in the economic plan of God, is not necessarily financial in nature and it is not necessarily meant to be stored away for future needs. Financial and material possessions are subject to deterioration, mold, and rot upon this earth and heaven has no need of any financial or earthly treasures.

The foremost important need is spiritual in nature. Often we are more focused on meeting financial and material needs, and cast spiritual needs aside as we come to the deserts of life, reaching instead for temporary worldly goods that quickly melt away as the heat of trials are turned up a notch or two.

God always sees and clearly knows our needs, the motives in our heart, and blesses us accordingly, here on this earth and even more so splendidly in heaven to come.

FOR FURTHER CONTEMPLATION:

Are you in the business of storing earthly treasures here on earth where they are destroyed by rot, rust, and mold? Or are you stacking up spiritual treasures and yearning towards that eternal home in Heaven?

What's the Difference?
Oppression of a Soul - Invasion of a Soul

Jesus answered, He it is, to whom I shall give a sop, when I have dipped it. And when he had dipped the sop, he gave it to Judas Iscariot, the son of Simon. And after the sop Satan entered into him. Then said Jesus unto him, That thou doest, do quickly. (John 13:26-27 KJV)

The vast spiritual arena surrounding us, including both light and dark forces, cannot be seen or completely understood in this present world. This spiritual realm is not to be taken lightly or joked about. These spiritual forces are real, exist in great number, and are powerful; but only as prevailing as the Lord allows. These evil forces are unable to be omini-present and omnipotent, as the Lord prevails. He exists everywhere always and both evil and light forces are ever subject to His authority and power.

For God hath not given us the spirit of fear; but of power, and of love, and of a sound mind. (2 Timothy 1:7 KJV)

God created us to be filled with the Holy Spirit's power of illuminating spiritual light, love, and free of opposing spiritual forces and darkness. This illuminating light, once alive or quickened inside us, gives us spiritual breath in our soul and awakens us to be of a sound mind; free from satanic invasion or oppression and spiritual harassment, freeing us to be about the business of our Lord as we walk in obedience to Him.

In whom ye also trusted, after that ye heard the word of truth, the gospel of your salvation: in whom also after that ye believed, ye were sealed with that holy Spirit of promise, Which is the earnest of our inheritance until the redemption of the purchased possession, unto the praise of his glory.(Ephesians 1:13-14 KJV)

Any soul awakened by the Holy Spirit is kept sealed by the Lord. An evil spirit cannot enter into a quickened soul and likewise the Holy Spirit cannot exit this same soul. All souls who have been saved are sealed until the day Jesus Christ redeems us; either by His return in the clouds or by natural death of the soul. This sealing of our souls is a "down payment" or earnest towards eternal life in Heaven and cannot be broken by anything we do or neglect to do here on earth. Salvation and sealing of our soul is a work of Jesus Christ and has nothing to do with a work of man; therefore man cannot ever lose our salvation. Man can grieve the Holy Spirit by being out of fellowship with Him. Eternal life means salvation is for eternity, not until we sin too much (how much sin would be too much sin causing us to lose our salvation anyways?)

And I give unto them eternal life; and they shall never perish, neither shall any man pluck them out of my hand. (John 10:28 KJV)

Because salvation is a work of Christ and not of man; one person cannot cause another to fall out of a salvation relationship with God. Again, salvation is all about God working in us and not about any works of man to earn salvation.

Soul(s) that exist under the invasion of dark spiritual evil forces, satanic in nature, are completely taken over by this opposing evil spirit(s). These spirits are operating against or in direct opposition to the things of the Lord. This is a spiritual catastrophe to the soul, or death of the soul. The presence of God is not alive and dwelling inside. This is a first class ticket to the execution of evil works and a passport straight to the fires of Hell at physical natural death.

Invasion of a soul such as this by dark spiritual forces can only happen to a soul of an unsaved person. A saved person can be oppressed or held down, but not invaded inwardly, by dark spiritual forces. An oppressed soul is a saved soul which becomes weighted down and overly burdened with the many cares of this world. Satan loves to keep people looking back over their shoulder, instead of looking up to Christ, and weighted down by the chains of sin from their past.

While I was with them in the world, I kept them in thy name: those that thou gavest me I have kept, and none of them is lost, but the son of perdition; that the scripture might be fulfilled. (John 17:12 KJV)

Judas had an evil spirit enter into him, a satanic invasion, as he shared bread with Jesus. Jesus discerned the very instant this evil force entered into the soul of Judas. Jesus already knew the works Judas was to complete. Jesus bid him to go about his work, orchestrating the events as they were to unfold, and fulfilling prophecy.

Judas died a selfish death, choosing to be cowardly and hanging himself after correlating the arrest and events leading up to the trial and death of Jesus together. For a mere thirty pieces of silver, Judas chose the works of evil forces and death, rather than coming to the end of himself and unto faith in Jesus Christ through accepting His free gift of salvation in faith.

Please take note: Judas followed in close association of Jesus Christ as He went about His ministry here on the earth. Judas heard the truth preached often, witnessed many miracles, maybe even professed his faith to others, or preached to others, but in the end chose to die without eternal salvation and to a certain final destiny in Hell for eternity.

FOR FURTHER CONTEMPLATION:

Have you allowed yourself to be oppressed by the cares of this world and the mud of your past sin and not spiritually available to be a walking billboard proclaiming the message of salvation through faith in Jesus Christ?

Or worse yet are you doomed and destined to the fires of Hell because you have never accepted the free gift of salvation through faith in Jesus Christ?

Today is the day of salvation; get your soul right with Jesus Christ today.

Noah's Ark

And God said unto Noah, The end of all flesh is come before me; for the earth is filled with violence through them; and, behold, I will destroy them with the earth. Make thee an ark of gopher wood; rooms shalt thou make in the ark, and shalt pitch it within and without with pitch. And this is the fashion which thou shalt make it of: The length of the ark shall be three hundred cubits, the breadth of it fifty cubits, and the height of it thirty cubits. A window shalt thou make to the ark, and in a cubit shalt thou finish it above; and the door of the ark shalt thou set in the side thereof; with lower, second, and third stories shalt thou make it. And, behold, I, even I, do bring a flood of waters upon the earth, to destroy all flesh, wherein is the breath of life, from under heaven; and every thing that is in the earth shall die. But with thee will I establish my covenant; and thou shalt come into the ark, thou, and thy sons, and thy wife, and thy sons' wives with thee. And of every living thing of all flesh, two of every sort shalt thou bring into the ark, to keep them alive with thee; they shall be male and female. Of fowls after their kind, and of cattle after their kind, of every creeping thing of the earth after his kind, two of every sort shall come unto thee, to keep them alive. And take thou unto thee of all food that is eaten, and thou shalt gather it to thee; and it shall be for food for thee, and for them. Thus did Noah; according to all that God commanded him, so did he. And the LORD said unto Noah, Come thou and all thy house into the ark; for thee have I seen righteous before me in this generation. (Genesis 6:13-7:1KJV)

The ark Noah prepared for the saving of his house is one of the most beautiful types or pictures of salvation to be found in the entire Bible.

How is salvation like Noah's ark?

The ark was not Noah's idea.

God said to Noah in **(Genesis 6:14 KJV) Make thee an ark of gopher wood."** God gave Noah specific instructions as to how to build it, the kind of wood to use, the size it should be, and where the door and window should be placed.

Salvation, like the ark, is a divine provision. It is not an after-thought of God. Long before man sinned God provided a plan of salvation. **(Revelation 13:8 KJV)** says

"Jesus Christ was ". . . the Lamb slain from the foundation of the world." Knowing that man was going to sin, God in the Person of Jesus Christ provided a means for us to be saved.

The ark was a divine provision. Salvation is also a divine provision. Salvation is not man reaching up to God but God reaching down to man. Religion, on the other hand, is man reaching up to God. You don't spell salvation "do"; you spell it "done."

A little boy came to an old preacher and asked, "What can I do to be saved?" The preacher answered "Son, you're too late." "What!" exclaimed the boy? "Too late to be saved?" "Oh, no," said the preacher, "not too late to be saved, but too late to do anything. Jesus did it all two thousand years ago."

The Bible states in *(John 1:13 KJV)* *"Which were born, not of blood, nor of the will of the flesh, nor of the will of man, but of God."*

And according to **(Titus 3:5 KJV) it is "Not by works of righteousness which we have done, but according to his mercy he saved us."**

The ark was a shelter from God's judgment.

God's judgment came on the world in the form of rain. It rained forty days and nights, flooding the whole earth. The rain fell but those inside the ark felt not a single drop, for they were protected by its shelter.

Two thousand years ago at Calvary the judgment of God fell, not in the form of rain, but in the form of separation from God. When God turned His back on Jesus, He cried out from the cross in *(Matthew 27:46 KJV)* we read *"And about the ninth hour Jesus cried with a loud voice, saying, Eli, Eli, lama sabachthani? that is to say, My God, my God, why hast thou forsaken me?"* God turned His back on Jesus Christ as the judgment of God fell on Jesus. While Jesus hung on the cross, God treated Him in exactly the same way He will have to treat every unbelieving sinner.

On the cross Jesus was suffering the sinner's judgment for sin. We were judged in Christ as a sinner two thousand years ago at Calvary, and God treated Jesus Christ like He would have to treat us if I did not trust Jesus Christ as my personal Saviour. When we trust Him, we are justified, cleared from all guilt. Jesus Christ, bore our guilt: He suffered our Hell; He paid our debt.

Those inside the ark were sheltered from God's judgment. The judgment fell on the ark, not on those inside. The person trusting Jesus Christ as personal Saviour is in the place of shelter from God's judgment, because the judgment fell on Jesus Christ at Calvary.

What is the significance of Noah and his family being invited into the ark?

God said to Noah in *(Genesis 7:1 KJV)* *"And the LORD said unto Noah, Come thou and all thy house into the ark; for thee have I seen righteous before me in this generation."*

I am told that invitational work **"come"** is found more than 1,900 times in the Bible. The Bible's last invitation is in (***Revelation 22:17 KJV***) *"And the Spirit and the bride say, Come. And let him that heareth say, Come. And let him that is athirst come. And whosoever will, let him take the water of life freely."*

Jesus said in *(**Matthew 11:28 KJV**) "Come unto me, all ye that labour and are heavy laden, and I will give you rest."*

Over and over again you are invited to come to Christ. God invited Noah in *(**Genesis 7:1 KJV**) "And the LORD said unto Noah, Come thou and all thy house into the ark . . ."* He did not say, "Noah, go into the ark." God was already inside. He had given it a "pre-float safety inspection."

God was in Christ Jesus reconciling the world unto Himself **(2 Cor. 5:19 KJV)**. Today he invites you to come and trust Him as Saviour. And anyone can come.

The ark only had one door.

The ark had only one door. Jesus said in *(**John 10:9 KJV**) "I am the door: by me if any man enter in, he shall be saved."* In John 14:6 *"Jesus saith unto him, I am the way, the truth, and the life: no man cometh unto the*

Father, but by me." Christ is the only door to Heaven, the only entrance.

There was not one door for the common cat and another for the lion, the king of the jungle. Everything that rode the ark to safety had to go in the same door.

Everyone was safe who entered into the ark.

No one entered the ark lost his life. The man who trusts Jesus Christ as Saviour is safe. Some who have trusted Christ are nervous, hoping to make it. They are nervous about their security. But, if you have trusted Jesus Christ as your Saviour, you are absolutely safe and enclosed in the palm of His hand.

When Noah and his family entered the ark, God shut the door, and no matter how bad the storm raged outside they were safe. We are safe in the arm of Jesus. The Bible says in ***(Ephesians 5:30 KJV) "For we are members of his body, of his flesh, and of his bones."***

What a beautiful picture of salvation! Won't you listen to Jesus Christ's invitation and come?

(Acts 16:30-31 KJV) "Sirs, what must I do to be saved? And they said, Believe on the Lord Jesus Christ, and thou shalt be saved, and thy house.

FOR FURTHER CONTEMPLATION:

Won't you come into the security of the ark?

Salvation is Simple

But I fear, lest by any means, as the serpent beguiled Eve through his subtilty, so your minds should be corrupted from the simplicity that is in Christ." (2 Corinthians 11:3 KJV)

Salvation it is so simple, yet multifaceted. It is more intricate than simply escaping a horrible death in Hell for all eternity. At the point of physical death a saved person's spirit is immediately escorted by angels and carried unto God's throne in heaven. The death of an unsaved person transports them immediately into to Hell for an eternity of horrible suffering and pain.

Salvation is not simply waving a magic wand and instantaneously living in a new life in Christ. The plan of salvation is intricate and detailed, encompassing deliverance from sin, peace with God, deliverance from the penalty of sin, and the presence of the Holy Spirit in one's life. There is nothing magical about salvation. Salvation is a miraculous intervention by a holy Christ into man's lost sinful natural condition of the heart.

"For by grace are ye saved through faith; and that not of yourselves: it is the gift of God: Not of works, lest any man should boast. For we are his workmanship,

created in Christ Jesus unto good works, which God hath before ordained that we should walk in them." (Ephesians 2:8-10 KJV)

Salvation is not brought about by any works. Man cannot earn a seat in the bleachers of Heaven. Salvation is a gift from God; it is a positional standing in the righteousness of Christ requiring no work or accomplishments on our part. Salvation is all about a holy God and what He did for us and nothing to do with any works of man. Salvation is not brought about by our good deeds or obedience to laws. Baptism does not bring about salvation or the thief on the cross would have missed out on a heavenly home in paradise with Christ. The thief accepted salvation by faith while hanging at death's door and was never baptized. This last minute salvation proves it is never too late to accept this gift of salvation; but in the same light- the sooner a person accepts this free gift it gives more time to do the will of God in this world as we sojourn upon this earth.

Salvation is a work of the Holy Spirit who prods us to accept Him. Our heavenly rewards are built upon our life of faith and obedience in this world. The sooner a person chooses to accept Christ in faith, the more time for him to accumulate treasures and eternal rewards in Heaven. All who are joined to Jesus Christ through faith will be rewarded according to their good works and obedience instead of facing judgment and eternal punishment of Hell where works of hay straw and wood will be burnt up and consumed in the fire.

Salvation is an inward change in a person's spiritual condition which works its way to the outer shell of each person. Man is spiritually alive the very moment he succumbs to the Holy Spirit's call or holy invitation to live inside a newly softened and yielding heart. A heart set apart from those who choose to continue in tune with the god of this world. The Holy Spirit sends invitations out to all to gain access into all hearts of those who are willing to open the door of their heart.

My little children, these things write I unto you, that ye sin not. And if any man sin, we have an advocate with the Father, Jesus Christ the righteous: And he is the propitiation for our sins: and not for ours only, but also for the sins of the whole world. (1 John 2:1-2 KJV)

The essence of Salvation includes one's own attorney or advocate, Jesus Christ, who speaks directly with The "Top Righteous Judge" in the Heavenly Supreme Court system; pleading our own sinful case and crying upon our behalf.

And because ye are sons, God hath sent forth the Spirit of his Son into your hearts, crying, Abba, Father. (Galatians 4:6 KJV)

The utmost characteristic of salvation is its free availability for all. Jesus did not pick and choose to die for only a select few men. Jesus chose to die upon the cross for all men. This paramount act of sacrificial love or gift of eternal life cost God the Father His only Son, who stamped out all sin debt and marked it "Paid in Full" for all sinners; past, present, and future. His work on the cross is finished, done, into the future.

For God so loved the world, that he gave his only begotten Son, that whosoever believeth in him should not perish, but have everlasting life. For God sent not his Son into the world to condemn the world; but that the world through him might be saved. (John 3:16-17 KJV)

The payment or satisfaction of all sin debt would be akin to Jesus not only making the down payment on your house, but going inside the bank and paying your entire mortgage in full, and paying the entire debt of your neighbors, family, friends, and strangers as well.

And I, if I be lifted up from the earth, will draw all men unto me. (John 12:32 KJV)

It is His great sacrificial love which acts or draws, as a magnet, beckoning all to consider His free gift and to accept it freely and simply. There are no individuals, groups, or certain sin, which disqualify any from receiving this free gift of eternal life. There is not an elect group or individuals who have been called and set apart to partake of salvation, exclusive of all other individuals. The gift is free for all who personally make a decision to partake of the spiritual relationship with Jesus Christ.

The only individuals who will not receive the gift of salvation and subsequently eternal life are those who do not accept with faith the blood of Jesus Christ shed for all sin. This is the unpardonable sin. My sins, your sins, and all sin have been covered and cancelled with His sacrificial payment of blood. Indeed, salvation is so simple and freely available to all who have faith. Many men stumble and fall over the simplicity of God's plan of salvation complicating it with many unnecessary factors and the red tape of divisive strange doctrines.

Study to shew thyself approved unto God, a workman that needeth not to be ashamed, rightly dividing the word of truth. (2 Timothy 2:15 KJV)

Many individuals not well grounded in the foundation and scriptural principles of God's Word get tangled up in a spider's web of various false belief systems, word definition deviations, and theological charades concerning salvation. Being utterly spiritually deficient and weak causes many to fail miserably. Many miss spending time alone with God in prayer and bible study, fail to compare and apply Truth in their life, and often miss the mark in rightly dividing God's Word in relation to His plan for salvation..

God's Word has always been intended to be clear-cut and defined, allowing each individual ample opportunity to appropriately interpret it and obediently live the "sold out life." If living this sacrificial life is impossible, God would not have already accomplished it through His Son, or asked all men to live accordingly as well.

I am crucified with Christ: nevertheless I live; yet not I, but Christ liveth in me: and the life which I now live in the flesh I live by the faith of the Son of God, who loved me, and gave himself for me. (Galatians 2:20 KJV)

Appearing before His judgment seat at death or at His return, no excuses will suffice, conceal, or camouflage any spiritual ineptness in our understanding of His unpretentious plan of salvation for all. We are all on equal footing at the cross and have been given all we need to live for Him.

FOR FURTHER CONTEMPLATION:

Have you accepted the free gift of salvation in your life? Or are you trying to earn your way in to Heaven's Holy Sanctuary by attaining your salvation via performances and achievements rooted in the god of this world?

In God's Waiting Room

Wait on the LORD: be of good courage, and he shall strengthen thine heart: wait, I say, on the LORD. (Psalms 27:14 KJV)

The world is fast paced and with savvy computerization of many tasks that were once loathsome and slow. There are numerous conveniences available to us today which have over time served to shorten our attention span and heightened our expectations of resolving situations in quick fashion. Most of us are not good at facing any circumstances where delays are common and highly inconvenient to our fast paced lifestyle.

There are delays at the airport due to circumstances of weather or safety which are out of our control. Delays are faced in physician's waiting rooms or other health care facilities while others ahead of us are receiving the quality of care we expect when our turn comes. There are frequently delays in being served our food in busy restaurants. This dilemma often leaves many hungry and irritable towards the waitress who cannot hurry the order along in the slow-moving kitchen. Life is full of "waiting room" opportunities.

When we do not receive answers quickly enough to our prayers we often give up and quit praying. We even resort to indirectly accusing God of failing to act on our behalf in the situation at hand. Delays in answering prayer are not necessarily denials from the hand of God.

God often tests our faith and strengthens us in waiting times. He leads us along the narrow path and into the "waiting rooms of life" as necessary for our spiritual growth. If we desire answers and blessings from God, most often we have to persevere in pursuing after them, while listening closely for His response. God does not often choose to glibly hand out sought after answers or special blessings to those who seek them half-heartedly or with the wrong spiritual attitude.

Parents often use the same manner of tabling a child's request until they know whether this child is truly sincere in his appeal and desire. This waiting period often helps to determine how important the request it is and how hard the child is willing to pursue it.

Yes, there are times when God answers our prayers immediately. He can even send the answer to our needs before we ask. Often we must learn the discipline of patience in the "waiting Rooms of life." In all situations the Bible instructs us to continue on in prayer:

Pray without ceasing. (1 Thessalonians 5:17 KJV)

The Bible also tells us to keep the power surging in our prayer life by keeping plugged into the real power source.

Confess your faults one to another, and pray one for another, that ye may be healed. The effectual fervent prayer of a righteous man availeth much. (James 5:16 KJV)

God often sets the answers to our prayers directly before us. Sometimes the answer we receive from God is not the answer we want to hear. This happened with Paul and removal of his thorn in the flesh, and Jesus in the Garden of Gethsemane. Paul and Jesus both chose to continue in their suffering, choosing to remain in the will of God, eternally focused on Him, and not upon their immediate suffering surrounding them.

Cast not away therefore your confidence, which hath great recompense of reward. For ye have need of patience, that, after ye have done the will of God, ye might receive the promise. (Hebrews 10:35-36 KJV)

FOR FURTHER CONTEMPLATION:

Are you in God's "waiting room" today? He does answer prayer to those who wait patiently for Him. Trust in God's answers He always has your best interests at heart even when the answer seems insurmountable in your own eyes.

Payment Of Sin

God Almighty has declared that sin must be paid for. What is the payment for sin? There can be no understanding or appreciation for the plan of salvation without understanding sin debt. This infinitely holy God has said that sin must be paid for. He said to Adam in **Genesis 2:17 "But of the tree of the knowledge of good and evil, thou shalt not eat of it: for in the day that thou eatest thereof thou shalt surely die." Romans 6:23 says "For the wages of sin is death."** And we read in

James 1:15 "sin, when it is finished, bringeth forth death." God almighty has declared that sin must be paid for. And the payment is death.

This death is more than physically dying with a gunshot wound or with cancer. It is described in **(Revelation 20:14 KJV)** as the second death. **"And death and hell were cast into the lake of fire. This is the second death."**

If I had to pay what I owe as a sinner, then I must die, go into Hell and stay there forever and ever. That's the price that God demands for my sins.

The Bible does not say the wages of sin is joining the church. Joining every church in town would not pay what I owe as a sinner.

The Bible does not say the wages of sin is being baptized. I could be baptized until every tadpole in the creek knew my Social Security number by memory, but that would not pay my sin debt.

The Bible does not say the wages of sin is turning over a new leaf. Reforming would not pay what I owe as a sinner.

The Bible does not say the wages of sin is performing good works. By working a thousand lifetimes, I still could not pay what I owe as a sinner.

The Bible says, **"The wages of sin is death."** God has one payment for sin, and that is an eternal death in the lake of fire. The only thing I can do to pay my debt is die, go into Hell and stay there forever.

The good news is Jesus already paid that price for us! All we have to do is accept the free gift of salvation.

(Romans 6:23 KJV) For the wages of sin is death; but the gift of God is eternal life through Jesus Christ our Lord.

(Romans 6:23 KJV) For the wages of sin is death; but the gift of God is eternal life through Jesus Christ our Lord.

(John 3:36 KJV) He that believeth on the Son hath everlasting life: and he that believeth not the Son shall not see life; but the wrath of God abideth on him.

(Isaiah 45:22 KJV) Look unto me, and be ye saved, all the ends of the earth: for I am God, and there is none else.

FOR FURTHER CONTEMPLATION:

Have you considered the eternal cost of your sin which is separation from God for all eternity unless you personally look unto God through the work of His Son Jesus Christ upon the cross at Calvary.

The Pride of the King

The king spake, and said, Is not this great Babylon, that I have built for the house of the kingdom by the might of my power, and for the honour of my majesty? (Daniel 4:30 KJV)

What overflowing pride came spewing forth from the mouth of King Nebuchadnezzar! He clamored, taking all credit for his great earthly kingdom. He boasted it was he who had engineered and built this empire. All accomplished in his own strength and power. The kingdom reverberated forth, uplifting his glory and honor.

God succinctly interrupted the king's ego:

While the word was in the king's mouth, there fell a voice from heaven, saying, O king Nebuchadnezzar, to thee it is spoken; The kingdom is departed from thee. And they shall drive thee from men, and thy dwelling shall be with the beasts of the field: they shall make thee to eat grass as oxen, and seven times shall pass over thee, until thou know that the most High ruleth in the kingdom of men, and giveth it to whomsoever he will. (Daniel4:31-32 KJV)

God spoke to King Nebuchadnezzar with resounding authority, squashing his alter ego and his control of this earthly kingdom came crashing down to an abrupt end. The earthly king was subject to the power and authority of the heavenly King, God, who rightly stripped his earthly ruling authority away.

Not only did King Nebuchadnezzar lose his reign but in short order he also lost his mind. He became as an animal or creature moving about upon the ground like an oxen without any human capabilities or reason.

The same hour was the thing fulfilled upon Nebuchadnezzar: and he was driven from men, and did eat grass as oxen, and his body was wet with the dew of heaven, till his hairs were grown like eagles' feathers, and his nails like birds' claws. And at the end of the days I Nebuchadnezzar lifted up mine eyes unto heaven, and mine understanding returned unto me, and I blessed the most High, and I praised and honoured him that liveth for ever, whose dominion is an everlasting dominion, and his kingdom is from generation to generation: (Daniel 4:33-34 KJV)

The Bible is not crystal clear on how long he remained as an animal without any human mental facilities. It does state at the end of his days, in old age; he lifted his eyes up to look upon heaven. The moment he chose to look upon heaven and acknowledge who God is, and his own detrimental physical and mental state, spiritual understanding came upon him. Nebuchadnezzar chose to honor God.

King Nebuchadnezzar found salvation in God near the end of his earthly life. Just like the thief on the cross would do on Calvary, as death stood near, he opened up the door to his heart.

FOR FURTHER CONTEMPLATION:

What about the door to your own heart? Is it open for the King of Kings to permeate every crack and crevice or is it bound with chains and shuttered up tightly as you wallow around in mud? Many today are in utter misery physically, emotionally, and mentally.

Keep thy heart with all diligence; for out of it are the issues of life. (Proverbs 4:23 KJV)

Pattern for Prayer

In Matthew Chapter 6 Jesus teaches us three practical things regarding prayer:

Prayer must come from the heart and not from the lips.

(Matthew 6:7 KJV) "But when ye pray, use not vain repetitions, as the heathen do: for they think that they shall be heard for their much speaking."

The Bible is not forbidding a person from praying the same prayer over and over again. It is forbidding using words out of habit without any meaning from the heart.

Prayer is not meant to change God as much as to change us.

(Matthew 6:8 KJV) "Be not ye therefore like unto them: for your Father knoweth what things ye have need of, before ye ask him."

Prayer was never designed to inform God of what He did not already know but rather to be a tool whereby we would be changed as we got to know Him more.

Prayer has definite qualities. It is primarily for Christians.

(Matthew 6:9 KJV) "After this manner therefore pray ye: Our Father which art in heaven, Hallowed be thy name."

That is not to say that God cannot hear the prayer of the lost, for He is waiting to hear the cry of repentance. And the rich man in hell's prayer was heard – but it was not answered.

Jesus also provides us with five different qualities of prayer,

It is primarily for Christians.

Prayer requires a right attitude about God's holiness.

(Matthew 6:9 KJV) "After this manner therefore pray ye: Our Father which art in heaven, Hallowed be thy name."

Prayer that gets results is going to have to recognize the holiness of God and sinfulness of man.

Prayer requires a right attitude about God's will.

(Matthew 6:10 KJV) "Thy kingdom come. Thy will be done in earth, as it is in heaven."

When praying we must always surrender our will to whatever the ultimate plan is that God has for our lives as well as for this world.

Prayer is asking for definite things.

(Matthew 6:11 KJV) "Give us this day our daily bread."

Prayer is not flowery language spoken to tell God how to do His job. It is His appointed way of getting what we need by asking specifically for those things in faith.

Prayer requires a right relationship with others.

(Matthew 6:14-15 KJV) "For if ye forgive men their trespasses, your heavenly Father will also forgive you: But if ye forgive not men their trespasses, neither will your Father forgive your trespasses."

God very wisely ties His answers to our willingness to keep right with others. If we refuse to forgive others, then we will have our prayers hindered until we choose to get right.

Finally, in Matthew Chapter 6 Jesus teaches us what we need to know for today about fasting.

Jesus expects Christians to fast. Pay close attention to what it says

(Matthew 6:16a KJV) "Moreover when ye fast."

We notice here that Jesus did not say IF but WHEN ye fast.

Fasting is tied to the attitude of the heart.

(Matthew 6:16 KJV) "Moreover when ye fast, be not, as the hypocrites, of a sad countenance: for they disfigure their faces, that they may appear unto men to fast. Verily I say unto you, They have their reward."

The one element that was missing in the fast of the Pharisees was a pure motive. They were trying to please men instead of God.

Fasting should be done in secret.

(Matthew 6:17-18 KJV) "But thou, when thou fastest, anoint thine head, and wash thy face; That thou appear not unto men to fast, but unto thy Father which is in secret: and thy Father, which seeth in secret, shall reward thee openly."

This is not saying that no one can be allowed to know that one is fasting, for family members would probably know. A few close friends may know as well. The idea is that it is not to be broadcast in general.

FOR FURTHER CONSIDERATION:

Prayer is important to God and important to having a right spiritual relationship with Him. The Bible has much to say about prayer.

Can Woman Preach?

If somebody asked you "why can't a woman be a preacher?" Would you have a biblical based reply?

Many churches today have women serving as preachers of the flock; but is allowing this scriptural? For God's answer to this we have we have a reliable and sure place we can search for the answer.

Let's look at the Bible and see what God has to say.....

This is a true saying, If a man desire the office of a bishop, he desireth a good work. A bishop then must be blameless, the husband of one wife, vigilant, sober, of good behaviour, given to hospitality, apt to teach; Not given to wine, no striker, not greedy of filthy lucre; but patient, not a brawler, not covetous; One that ruleth well his own house, having his children in subjection

with all gravity; (For if a man know not how to rule his own house, how shall he take care of the church of God?) Not a novice, lest being lifted up with pride he fall into the condemnation of the devil. Moreover he must have a good report of them which are without; lest he fall into reproach and the snare of the devil. (1Timothy 3:1-7 KJV)

It seems many still ask this question "why can't a woman be pastor?" In our modern society one of the biggest spiritual issues is about people not understanding a woman's role in regards to God's church. The text from 1 Timothy provides God's requirements for pastoring in a church. Note what it states in verse two the bishop must be the husband of one wife. Also note in verse 4 he must rule HIS house well. In verse 5 it says if a MAN does not know how to rule his house well, how shall he take care of the church. In verse 6 and 7 the scripture states it mentions HE again.

Note in verse 2 the pastor needs to be apt to teach. This means that the pastor should be able and ready to teach. In

(1 Timothy 2:12 KJV) we read "But I suffer not a woman to teach, nor to usurp authority over the man, but to be in silence."

This verse clearly states that a woman is not to usurp authority over man or to teach men.

Clearly as these verses teach the reason women are not to teach is based or founded within God's Word and clearly should be our answer to those who ask why a why a woman cannot be a preacher, it is because as the qualifications as given in scripture, they do not qualify.

FOR FURTHER CONTEMPLATION:

Read **Titus 1:6-16** for more insight and spiritual discernment about God's qualifications for pastoring a church.

Death of a Pet

Humans all have to reconcile with death one day. The Bible is very clear on this:

And as it is appointed unto men once to die, but after this the judgment: (Hebrews 9:27 KJV)

It will be physical death unto the heat of Hell or unto spiritual eternal life in Heaven singing and praising God at His throne in Heaven.

Then shall the dust return to the earth as it was: and the spirit shall return unto God who gave it." (Ecclesiastes 12:7 KJV)

Animals and pets also die. Often people will make statements telling you they look forward to seeing their pet again "on the other side or "across the rainbow bridge" referring to an opportunity to see their pet again in eternity and believing in the certainty of this possibility in the present makes the loss and pain easier to digest for many pet owners.

The Bible states at death our human spirit goes to be with the Lord. Animals are not made or formed by God in His creation exactly like humans are. In Genesis God made man after his own image and animals after their own kind. Man has a spirit, a will, and a human body and is made a trichotomy.

Pets and animals on the other hand, do not have a spirit or will to choose to call upon the Lord in faith to be saved as a human, made after His image, can choose to do. Nowhere in the Bible does it implicitly state pets will be with us in Heaven. There are a few clues concerning animals.

First the Bible tells us:

But as it is written, Eye hath not seen, nor ear heard, neither have entered into the heart of man, the things which God hath prepared for them that love him. (1 Corinthians 2:9 KJV)

This verse tells us that no human can interpret and know exactly what will be included in heaven or what it will be like for those that are saved. Clearly Heaven is so grand, much grander than any can clearly see or speak about, that it is indescribable; maybe even ushering complete silence before the coming spiritual events of the end times. In Heaven before the seventh seal is opened there is silence for about a half an hour. Heaven is astonishing even from our limited earthly perspective.

"And when he had opened the seventh seal, there was silence in heaven about the space of half an hour." Revelation 8:1 KJV)

The Bible does speak about animals existing in heaven so undoubtedly animals will be in heaven but there is no indication that it will include animals previously alive on earth will also be in heaven.

"The wolf and the lamb shall feed together, and the lion shall eat straw like the bullock: and dust shall be the serpent's meat. They shall not hurt nor destroy in all my holy mountain, saith the LORD."

From the perspective of earth we are looking through the glass darkly. Until we get to see heaven with our own eyes and experience the atmosphere and joyous singing we will all partake in nobody will know for sure just how glorious it will be.

"For now we see through a glass, darkly; but then face to face: now I know in part; but then shall I know even as also I am known." (1 Corinthians 13:12 KJV)

FOR FURTHER CONTEMPLATION:

We know for sure a new heaven and new earth will exist in eternity from our human knowledge but we cannot fathom how wonderful it will be or precisely what we may find there.

A Prayerless Nation

Seek ye the LORD while he may be found, call ye upon him while he is near: (Isaiah 55:6 KJV)

The devil has little to fear prowling around seeking individuals he can overwhelm, confound, and bury in doubt and fear. Many are living a rushed existence, struggling to provide for their family, living defeated lives, lacking hope, seeking love, consumed with anger, worrying about the state of our nation, and drowning in heaps of stress.

Prayerless churches, prayerless bible studies, prayerless homes, and prayerless schools. The devil is having a heyday in our prayerless and powerless nation. We have become unplugged, undone, and far removed from there only real source of power. Jesus Christ is the everlasting power source.

Until a person intimately recognizes their circumstances are utterly helpless, prayer seems like an option on the shelf instead of an avenue offering a ray hope. One must perceive themselves through the eyes of a holy Lord not through the rose colored glasses the world wears.

The application of the above verse in Isaiah is foremost to Israel and the Jewish people in the day and time of the Lord's return. However, the verse can also be applied to our nation and her numerous woes today.

"If my people, which are called by my name, shall humble themselves, and pray, and seek my face, and turn from their wicked ways; then will I hear from heaven, and will forgive their sin, and will heal their land." (2 Chronicles 7:14 KJV)

The Lord desires and yearns to bless His own children of the Jewish heritage, and by spiritual adoption, Gentiles as well.

The Lord placed conditions upon His blessing as stated in the above verse. The conditions are humbleness, prayer, repentance and turning away from wickedness. Today He still promises to heal the land as these specific conditions are met.

FOR FURTHER CONTEMPLATION:

We are a prayerless nation who needs to turn towards a powerful God amongst the wickedness surrounding us on every side. One day soon it will be too late to call upon the Lord.

The Truth Slices Like A Knife

For the word of God is quick, and powerful, and sharper than any twoedged sword, piercing even to the dividing asunder of soul and spirit, and of the joints and marrow, and is a discerner of the thoughts and intents of the heart. Neither is there any creature that is not manifest in his sight: but all things are naked and opened unto the eyes of him with whom we have to do. " (Hebrews 4:12-13 KJV)

Prominence is justly placed upon the sharpness of the truth of God's Word. This piercing blade of truth slices deep into the heart and soul of man as he reads God's Word with spiritually quickened eyes or hears scripture verses quoted through spiritually awakened ears. The Lord awakens whosoever reaches out in faith to Him, seizing onto His truth. This truth penetrates deep into the cracks and crevices of man's sinful heart once filled to the brim with spiritual ashes, dust and drought of one's once dark past.

Both sides of the edge of the knife are sharpened truth, honed for maximum effect on each forward and backward slice. Nothing is hidden or concealed from the Lord. His blade is molded of unapologetic truth, filleting or exposing sin, and cutting straight to the heart of the issues at hand outwardly and hidden in the inner realms.

This dividing or cutting to expose has been compared to the necessity of a scalpel for a surgeon performing an operation on a physical body. God's Word is critical, vital in maintaining a healthy and robust spiritual life.

The truth of His Word can be likened to tossing a life-preserver towards a brittle hard heart, struggling to stay afloat in the bitter ocean of life. Man is continuously being assaulted and overwhelmed by the waves of doubt, depression, addictions, trials and struggles of many varieties. His Truth never changes falters, or becomes overwhelmed in any situation. His Word carries us through, surfing upon the top of the waves of the world.

Jesus Christ the same yesterday, and to day, and for ever. (Hebrews 13:8 KJV)

FOR FURTHER CONTEMPLATION:

His truth never fails in preserving and softening a heart of stone. God's word cuts to the deepest level of human life.

Piloting a Hot Air Balloon

A balloon pilot strives to keep the balloon afloat in the lower atmosphere, just above earth. Ascending or descending as necessary by means of hot air. This hot air causes the balloon to rise in the cooler air of the atmosphere, or allows the hot air to dissipate as the balloon descends towards the ground. The hot air is heated by large propane burners at the bottom of the balloon and this air can be vented out at the top of the balloon as necessary, for lowering the temperature inside the balloon.

The pilot relies upon simple science to pilot his balloon. The balloon's flight is dependent upon the difference between the weight of warmer air inside the balloon versus the cooler air in the atmosphere. Warm air rises above cooler air sending the balloon floating upwards. Cooler air inside the balloon, as the warmer air escapes out of the top of the balloon causing the balloon to gently float downward in the atmosphere. The pilot's job is to keep the balloon aloft, ascending or descending as necessary along its flight path. Or to gently bringing it down to the ground at the end of the day's journey.

God's filling an individual with the Holy Spirit, or spiritual air, could be compared to a balloon pilot filling his balloon with hot air. This "holy hot air" a Christian receives from the Holy Spirit can send us, in His power, aloft over difficult situations we face, and descending down on our knees as necessary, keeping our spiritual atmosphere buoyant, sailing along the narrow path towards our future in eternity. The atmosphere surrounding us would be continually warmed by His infilling spirit, grace and truth, keeping us "in flight" for Him.

But the hour cometh, and now is, when the true worshippers shall worship the Father in spirit and in truth: for the Father seeketh such to worship him. God is a Spirit: and they that worship him must worship him in spirit and in truth." (John 4:23-24 KJV)

If a balloon pilot chose to fill the inside of the balloon entirely with cold air he would never achieve any lift off the ground. If a Christian attempts to live the Christian life by filling himself with powerless religiosity, wishful thinking, rituals, and a works religion, or even a sincere, but human, attempt at working out his Christian life he will never proclaim a true profession of faith, nor rise to a faithful and true dependence in Christ. The Christian life can only be lived by the true indwelling of the Holy Spirit. Any substitutes or "cold air" in our spiritual flight plan will not suffice in thrusting one along the journey towards eternity while living in this world, instead will keep one's flight stagnant and grounded in the things of this world.

The simple fact is true faith in Jesus Christ always produces spiritual fruit. Faith in Christ always produces the lift in the Christian life. If a person's "spiritual balloon" never separates from the ground, rising above the chaos of the world, then their faith is misplaced and their profession is in vain. Many profess to know Christ, and they do, but many only in their mind and not with saving faith in their heart. True faith in Jesus Christ always produces a change in the heart.

Keep thy heart with all diligence; for out of it are the issues of life. (Proverbs 4:23 KJV)

A Christian who is living this "sold out life" in his heart is not merely living a social gospel or a numbered profession in a mega church but is living daily, hourly, and by minute, sacrificing this temporary life for the glory and honor of Jesus Christ, soaring upward and onward, as a hot air balloon in flight, while sojourning here in this earthly life.

I beseech you therefore, brethren, by the mercies of God, that ye present your bodies a living sacrifice, holy, acceptable unto God, which is your reasonable service. And be not conformed to this world: but be ye transformed by the renewing of your mind, that ye may prove what is that good, and acceptable, and perfect, will of God. (Romans 12:1-2 KJV)

FOR FURTHER CONTEMPLATION:

Are you soaring for Jesus Christ while living in this world or does your spiritual flight need the strength and perseverance of holy wings of precious air?

A Rainbow of Promise

A Rainbow, with an emerald glow about it, surrounds the throne in heaven. This rainbow forms a complete circle. The apostle John saw the whole circle of God's great comfort and assurance firsthand. The throne was hedged roundabout with the brilliance of His divine promise. John was overcome by the sight of this royal throne and the magnificence of His presence. This illuminating rainbow surrounding the throne had a brilliant emerald hue. Straightway John fell to the floor in awe and humility in the presence of almighty God.

As the appearance of the bow that is in the cloud in the day of rain, so was the appearance of the brightness round about. This was the appearance of the likeness of the glory of the LORD. And when I saw it, I fell upon my face, and I heard a voice of one that spake. (Ezekiel 1:28 KJV)

And he that sat was to look upon like a jasper and a sardine stone: and there was a rainbow round about the throne, in sight like unto an emerald. (Revelation 4:3 KJV)

A half a rainbow, not a complete circle, can be found occasionally after a rain shower arching in the sky above our world. This rainbow is a sign, or covenant, from God promising never to flood the earth again as in the days of Noah.

And I will establish my covenant with you; neither shall all flesh be cut off any more by the waters of a flood; neither shall there any more be a flood to destroy the earth. And God said, This is the token of the covenant which I make between me and you and every living creature that is with you, for perpetual generations: I do set my bow in the cloud, and it shall be for a token of a covenant between me and the earth. And it shall come to pass, when I bring a cloud over the earth, that the bow shall be seen in the cloud: And I will remember my covenant, which is between me and you and every living creature of all flesh; and the waters shall no more become a flood to destroy all flesh. (Genesis 9:11-15 KJV)

The Science aspect of rainbows is clearly phenomenal. The sun shines through rain drops creating an awesome looking rainbow as refracting or bending of light rays with different colors traveling and bending at different speeds, and then these light rays mix with rain, creating a rainbow in the atmosphere. The colors bend or refract at different speeds and therefore God has even given each color a particular place in the curvature of a rainbow. Our God is a God of finite details.

A rainbow is a sign of God's longsuffering and covenant with His own children. He promised to never sending a flood as devastating as the one He sent in judgment of the wickedness abounding as in the days of Noah. The rainbow serves as a reminder of this covenant. It also vibrantly displays His willingness to be longsuffering so that many men can accept His free gift of salvation.

The rainbow also serves as a colorful warning to those who choose to live in wickedness. God has promised those who choose to continue living in wickedness will sin unto death, a death leading them to Hell.

Who will render to every man according to his deeds: To them who by patient continuance in well doing seek for glory and honor and immortality, eternal life: But unto them that are contentious, and do not obey the truth, but obey unrighteousness, indignation and wrath, Tribulation and anguish, upon every soul of man that doeth evil, of the Jew first, and also of the Gentile; But glory, honour, and peace, to every man that worketh good, to the Jew first, and also to the Gentile: For there is no   respect of persons with God. (Romans 2:6-11 KJV)

Some today choose to wickedly parade a rainbow flag as a logo or symbol for unnatural relations between men or between women, polluting the holiness of the scriptural meaning of God's rainbow. The rainbow is always a symbol of God's holy promise, never to be used as a sign of a wicked lifestyle of rebellion against God's holy and perfect relationship order of man. Man could not replenish the earth if employing unnatural relations in place of God's holy marriage union between a man and woman.

So God created man in his own image, in the image of God created he him; male and female created he them. And God blessed them, and God said unto them, Be fruitful, and multiply, and replenish the earth, and subdue it: and have dominion over the fish of the sea, and over the fowl of the air, and over every living thing that moveth upon the earth. (Genesis 1:27-28 KJV)

God's rainbow is always a symbol of His promise to His own. God is a holy God of intimate mercy, grace and truth. When the Christian witnesses a rainbow in the sky it is a reminder of God's covenant promise. To those who live in sin and wickedness a rainbow is a sign of God's imminent judgment of their sin and depravity.

FOR FURTHER CONTEMPLATION:

Do you see God's promise in the rainbow?

Hidden Manna and a white Stone

He that hath an ear, let him hear what the Spirit saith unto the churches; To him that overcometh will I give to eat of the hidden manna, and will give him a white stone, and in the stone a new name written, which no man knoweth saving he that receiveth it." (Revelation 2:17 KJV)

God promises hidden manna, a white stone, and a new name to those that are overcomers of this world and the devil, sharing in eternal victory with God with Jesus Christ at His right hand. To "cash in" on these promises one must crack open his Bible and glean the many truths and promises contained in scripture. This holy treasure hunting cannot be done by shallow reading, barely scratching the surface, in depth and persistent study is necessary and commanded by God.

Study to shew thyself approved unto God, a workman that needeth not to be ashamed, rightly dividing the word of truth. (2 Timothy 2:15 KJV)

Pondering and musing over His Word, in correlation with a saving relationship with Him, is essential in finding this hidden cache of manna. God has buried His manna, golden treasures or nuggets of truth, for those who are willing to dig deeply to discover them. These treasures unlock a deeper relationship with Jesus Christ for those willing to grab the shovel and dig.

In biblical times manna was the divine food of the Israelites, specially provided by God for their preservation as they trudged towards the Promised Land. Hidden manna was later placed in a pot and preserved in the Ark of the Covenant along with the Ten Commandments. This ark disappeared from man's possession and the ends of the earth, but later is mentioned in Revelation as being present in Heaven. In heaven, I persist in believing, all who are present with Him there will be given the deeper spiritual truth of this precious and divinely hidden manna whose understanding is reserved for His eternal Kingdom.

And the temple of God was opened in heaven, and there was seen in his temple the ark of his testament: and there were lightnings, and voices, and thunderings, and an earthquake, and great hail. (Revelation 11:19 KJV)

The white stone in biblical times was equated to having been declared NOT GUILTY. For example, in the Jewish Sanhedrin kangaroo court system a white stone was given by jurors when declaring NOT GUILTY to the one who was on trial. In contrast the black stone was given by these ancient jurors to declare one GUILTY as charged. Hence the term blackballed, you might hear one claim today when confirmed unanimously guilty. Because Jesus's died on the cross at Calvary, we have been given, at no cost to us, the white ball, or declared NOT GUILTY, in God's perfect court system.

A white stone is given to each of His sheep, as a gift of eternal life, for whosoever will believe and place his faith in Christ. This white stone contains a new name for each soul who has found the gift of salvation in Christ. Like Saul became known as Paul on the road to Damascus, each saved individual becomes known in The Good Shepherd's flock as a new person in Christ. This new name is written in the Lamb's Book of Life, for those who have faith, and this new name will be called forth one day to spend an eternity with Him.

For those individuals who have been "blackballed" or given the black stone by men on earth will reap eternal rewards in heaven according to God's fair and just scale of eternal judgment. Even in the times when it seems wicked prevails on Earth and that one has been with prejudice accused, God's justice will one day reward those who suffered unjustly for His glory while sojourning on Earth. The opposite side of this equation is that those who persist in wicked deeds will one day reap their rewards accordingly.

He that overcometh, the same shall be clothed in white raiment; and I will not blot out his name out of the book of life, but I will confess his name before my Father, and before his angels. (Revelation 3:5 KJV)

Let them be blotted out of the book of the living, and not be written with the righteous. (Psalms 69:28 KJV)

The contrasting consequence of not being written in the Lamb's Book of Life is to be given the black ball, or condemned to a life in Hell. Either a person is headed for eternal life with Christ or heading towards the deep hot pit of Hell.

And whosoever was not found written in the book of life was cast into the lake of fire. (Revelation 20:15 KJV)

And the LORD said unto Moses, Whosoever hath sinned against me, him will I blot out of my book. Therefore now go, lead the people unto the place of which I have spoken unto thee: behold, mine Angel shall go before thee: nevertheless in the day when I visit I will visit their sin upon them. (Exodus 32:33-34 KJV)

FOR FURTHER CONTEMPLATION:

Have you been given the white stone of eternal promises and your name placed in the Book of Life? Or are you heading down the path towards Hell?

Have you been unjustly or unfairly accused by man, God will adjust the balances in eternity to those that overcome the world.

Hell is a Real Place

Today many have no conception of Hell, Sheol in the Hebrew, or Hades, Tartarus, and Gehenna in the Greek language. It is a literal place where men are in the process of dying but never succumbing to death, subjected to incessant agony and physical torment. Churches need to be unapologetic in preaching the clear biblical truth about Hell. Christians need to be able to witness about Heaven to others, and plainly delineating about the horror of an authentic place called Hell. All men must come to terms with an actual place called Hell and the hope of eternity with Christ.

The book of Revelation tells us "He has the keys to Hell and death." Life and death are in the power of His nail torn hands because His sacrificial death for our sins on the cross took away the power of death, giving us the gift of salvation and eternal life.

The following verse proves His deity over time; past, present and future, He is not bound or limited by time as man is. This verse plainly declares there is a literal heaven and likewise, or opposite, a literal hell.

I am he that liveth, and was dead; and, behold, I am alive for evermore, Amen; and have the keys of hell and of death. (Revelation 1:18 KJV)

Hell has been described as being a place that:

Man will have a memory that will NEVER fail.

It is a place that EVERY request will be denied.

It is a place of HATRED.

It is a place located DOWNWARD, NOT UPWARDS towards eternity

A place of Outer DARKNESS

A PRISON in chains

It is a place of UNQUENCHABLE THIRST, a thirst for spiritual things of Christ that can never be quenched.

It is a place of ever LONGING.

It is a place of FIRE that is NEVER extinguished.

A place where the worm DIETH NOT, sinners never die

A place of EVERLASTING DESTRUCTION.

A place of NO REST day and night.

A place of TORMENT day and night for eternity

Speaking about hell is not a popular subject in our society. Many deny its existence; others cannot fathom how a loving God could cast people into such a place. Though it may be unpopular and dated to speak of hell, the reality of its existence must be addressed and expounded upon. Just as one cannot deny the existence of God, or that He is the Creator of the world, it is also plainly stated in scripture about the existence of Hell.

And these shall go away into everlasting punishment: but the righteous into life eternal. (Matthew 25:46 KJV)

And they shall go forth, and look upon the carcasses of the men that have transgressed against me: for their worm shall not die, neither shall their fire be quenched; and they shall be an abhorring unto all flesh. (Isaiah 66:24 KJV)

Wherefore if thy hand or thy foot offend thee, cut them off, and cast them from thee: it is better for thee to enter into life halt or maimed, rather than having two hands or two feet to be cast into everlasting fire. (Matthew 18:8 KJV)

In flaming fire taking vengeance on them that know not God, and that obey not the gospel of our Lord Jesus Christ: Who shall be punished with everlasting destruction from the presence of the Lord, and from the glory of his power; (2 Thessalonians 1:8-9 KJV)

And the smoke of their torment ascendeth up for ever and ever: and they have no rest day nor night, who worship the beast and his image, and whosoever receiveth the mark of his name. (Revelation 14:11 KJV)

And it shall come to pass, that every soul, which will not hear that prophet, shall be destroyed from among the people. (Acts 3:23 KJV)

And shall cast them into the furnace of fire: there shall be wailing and gnashing of teeth. (Matthew 13:50 KJV)

And shall come forth; they that have done good, unto the resurrection of life; and they that have done evil, unto the resurrection of damnation. (John 5:29 KJV)

But I will forewarn you whom ye shall fear: Fear him, which after he hath killed hath power to cast into hell; yea, I say unto you, Fear him. (Luke 12:5 KJV)

Even as Sodom and Gomorrah, and the cities about them in like manner, giving themselves over to fornication, and going after strange flesh, are set forth for an example, suffering the vengeance of eternal fire. (Jude 1:7 KJV)

Behold, all souls are mine; as the soul of the father, so also the soul of the son is mine: the soul that sinneth, it shall die. (Ezekiel 18:4KJV)

FOR FURTHER CONTEMPLATION:

The scriptural confirmation for a place called Hell is overwhelming and certain for all mankind.

Likewise, the many promises and assurances of eternal life are bountiful, truthful, and freely available for whosoever has faith to believe in Him.

Choose peace and eternal life, not the wide road to Hell with its torment and heat hounding and taunting forever.

What Garment Adorns You?

Now Joshua was clothed with filthy garments, and stood before the angel. And he answered and spake unto those that stood before him, saying, Take away the filthy garments from him. And unto him he said, Behold, I have caused thine iniquity to pass from thee, and I will clothe thee with change of raiment. (Zechariah 3:3-4 KJV)

The world places a great emphasis on outward appearance, often neglecting their inner spiritual heart condition. People often choose to either adorn themselves with the latest and greatest fashions or choose to dress down themselves in grunge attire. Both are taking outer appearance to the extreme in worldly fashion and neither are necessarily honoring to God.

Joshua was clothed in filthy garments before the angel. Does this mean he took on the grungy look common to many in a younger mindset geared to the world's popular opinion and fashion trends? No, Joshua's filthy garments were an inner indication of a spiritual blight, not first and foremost an issue with His outer attire.

Joshua's heart was filled with sin. Sin is an evil ogre in the sight of the Lord and His angels. All sin must be properly addressed and dealt with according to the truth of God's Word. Nobody can come into the presence of the Lord with a sinful condition in their heart, as He is holy and perfect and knows no sin. Salvation adorns the sinner in a new white robe, a Christ like garment.

The Lord promised Joshua a change of raiment. That promise of obtaining new raiment or a new covering, or propitiation, is available today for any man, woman, or child who asks in faith. Whosoever calls upon Him in faith can have that new covering. Saving faith in the atoning work of Christ changes our inner heart condition from wicked and sinful to adorning us in freedom from sin and liberty in Christ.

And it shall come to pass, that whosoever shall call on the name of the Lord shall be saved. (Acts 2:21 KJV)

This new raiment is a spiritual covering for desperately wickedness and sin in man's heart and not a new outer shell or covering for the physical body. However, once this raiment begins to seep through this softened heart it also affects a person's outer persona and actions as the fruits of the spirit are manifested in the Christian's life.

Yes, the Lord is intimately concerned about our inner heart condition, more so than our outward presentation. However, both the inner heart condition and the outer shell of the Christian life are important. One involves our honest presentation before the Lord, and the other is how the Christian is viewed by others, as he navigates through the world. The inner state of a man's heart can be vastly different from how he chooses to present himself to those around him but the Lord always knows the true condition of our heart. What does your heart condition look like to the Lord?

FOR FURTHER CONTEMPLATION:

The Lord always intimately knows the spiritual condition of your heart. Does your heart personify an aroma of Jesus Christ in, on and about yourself to Him and to others around you? Or do you need a new garment?

Calling the Church

If we confess our sins, he is faithful and just to forgive us our sins, and to cleanse us from all unrighteousness. (1 John 1:9 KJV)

Behold, I stand at the door, and knock: if any man hear my voice, and open the door, I will come in to him, and will sup with him, and he with me. (Revelation 3:20 KJV)

"Behold, I Stand at the Door and Knock." These words are generally quoted as an appeal to sinners, but they are not, in context they are addressed to a Church, a Church in whose midst Christ had once stood, but now found Himself excluded; standing outside knocking for admittance.

This is one of the most startling things recorded in the New Testament, that it is possible for a church to be outwardly prosperous and yet have no Christ in its midst, and be unconscious of the fact. This is a description of a Church without Christ. Excluded from His own nation, for they rejected Him; excluded from the world, for it crucified Him; excluded from His Church, for He stands outside its door knocking for Entrance.

How did Christ come to be outside the Church? He had been within it once or there never would have been a Church. How did He come to leave? It is clear that they had not thrust Him out, for they do not seem to have missed His presence. They continued to worship Him, to sing His praises, and engage in all manner of Christian service, yet He had withdrawn. Why? The reason is summed up in one word--Worldliness.

But how is Christ to get back into His Church? Does it require the unanimous vote or invitation of the membership? No. "If any man hear my voice, and open the door, I will come in to him, and will sup with him, and he with Me." That is the way to revive a lukewarm church is for the individual members to open their hearts and let Christ re-enter, and thus open the door for His reappearance.

The character of many Church today is Laodicean, and as this period continues until the Church of the "New-Born" is taken out, we cannot hope for any great change until the Lord comes back.

FOR FURTHER CONTEMPLATION:

Is Christ dwelling in your church?

A Helpmeet For Man

And the LORD God said, It is not good that the man should be alone; I will make him an help meet for him. (Genesis 2:18 KJV)

The Creator God intimately anticipated all need and desires of man. He fashioned man with certain innate longings. Man was intricately molded by the hands of God to have need of a help meet, or companion.

The help meet was fashioned to fulfill or live up to these desires becoming one with man, intimately sharing in fellowship together; physically and spiritually in connection to God. God created man and woman for this relationship and fulfilling a perfect submissive union of man to woman and co- enjoined in a perfect triangle or union with Christ.

And God blessed them, and God said unto them, Be fruitful, and multiply, and replenish the earth, and subdue it: and have dominion over the fish of the sea, and over the fowl of the air, and over every living thing that moveth upon the earth. ***(Genesis 1:28 KJV)***

God blessed this perfect union calling for the union to consist of one man and woman who are fruitful in their spiritual life multiplying with a quiver full of children to fulfill the commandment to replenish the earth. Woman was created specifically to be the helpmeet or perfect companion of man.

Since the creation of this perfect and holy relationship pattern man and his helpmeet have lost their way from fulfilling or completing this triune union between God, man, and his wife. Man and woman both have mislaid or set aside godly desires for bringing their god honoring relationship to fruition, filling those innate desires instead with ungodly relations and things of this world. Many have lost the desire for a spiritual relationship connection between help meet, man and glued together through faith and the holy adhesive in a relationship with God through the selfish promotion of ambitions and a worldly ambitions in life that fulfill the desires of the god of this world instead of the will and holy way of God.

"I can bring home the bacon and fry it up in the pan", is a line from a popular jingle written for an eighties commercial for Enjoli perfume. This little catchy tune implies this women was highly satisfied, fulfilled and successful working outside the home for many hours earning bacon, and keep her house in working order, and keeping her man satisfied. This is the world's idea of how women, marriage, and home-life function. This is in direct conflict with God's perfect design who clearly states the man is to be the head of the home as he aligns himself under the umbrella of a spiritual relationship with God and likewise a God honoring relationship with his wife.

God laid out in His Word the perfect pattern to follow in cultivating the perfect marriage and household should function. Just as Joshua so emphatically stated in Joshua 24:15 "But as for me and my house we will serve the Lord." Man can resolutely determine and stand steadfastly in that very same outline in their home molded after God today. It begins by the man, as head of the house, serving the Lord with all his heart, and respectively his help meet and family circumstances shall fall into place behind his leading, as the Lord has determined.

Many men are absent, by choice, from their homes and family today. Not taking upon themselves to heed God's Word and are absent from fulfilling their duties as God intended. Women are finding worldly satisfaction in careers and jobs and are like- wise absent, by choice, from their divinely appointed place in the home. Money and greed, satisfaction and worldly desires, and misplaced priorities have severely weakened the triune union of God, man and his helpmeet, and furthermore have led to the shaking and crumbling foundations of marriage and quality family life in today's faltering society.

Men, take your place at the head of your family, in front of God, and in leadership of your home. Women, serve as help meet to your husband as you serve God first in holy union. Setting these priorities in your walk with God, your marriage, and your home, will raise up children who understand we serve a holy God who commands, through a loving relationship, that He comes first in our lives. Setting these standards in your own life can impact the succeeding generations bringing honor and glory to God.

By not adopting these holy standards God has set forth for us in His Word you are choosing to serve the devil. This allows our world to continually spiral towards destruction. Destruction from within, destruction of marriages, destruction of homes, destruction of families, and ultimately death as the devil is further lifted up and exalted by those who choose to follow after his wicked and deceiving lies instead of God's holy blueprints for our lives.

FOR FURTHER CONTEMPLATION:

What god do you choose to serve as you pass through this world the god or author of death and destruction?

Or do you follow The God of peace and joy and of the promise of eternal life?

Guarded On All Sides

Thus saith the LORD, thy Redeemer, the Holy One of Israel; I am the LORD thy God which teacheth thee to profit, which leadeth thee by the way that thou shouldest go." (Isaiah 48:17 KJV)

The Lord places a hedge about His sheep as they roam about in "fields" of life, like a shepherd who guards His own sheep against wolves and other predators who cunningly seek to devour any who profess the Truth of God's Word. The Lord guards and protects His sheep on all sides against the wiles of the devil and his dark cohorts.

The wiles of the devil include but are not limited to promoting false teaching and other harmful heresies which they often try to whisper in unsuspecting ears and work towards infiltrating the minds of those who are at rest in the darkness of the world.

In the setting of evening as the darkness enfolds around them the shepherd herds his sheep into the sheep fold for the night just as our Lord gathers us into His arms as spiritual darkness begins to envelope itself around us. He protects His own children from: "principalities, against powers, against the rulers of the darkness of this world, against spiritual wickedness in high places..."

And the LORD went before them by day in a pillar of a cloud, to lead them the way; and by night in a pillar of fire, to give them light; to go by day and night: (Exodus 13:21 KJV)

And the LORD, he it is that doth go before thee; he will be with thee, he will not fail thee, neither forsake thee: fear not, neither be dismayed."   (Deuteronomy 31:8 KJV)

In every situation God goes before us filtering obstacles from inhibiting our pathway; removing problematic obstacles and clearing the way as He deems necessary for our spiritual health and growth.

For the Israelites journey to the Promised Land He provided a pillar of cloud before them by day and fire by night to guide them as they marched in the desert for forty years. Sometimes they marched about in circles as they headed towards the Promised Land, but God was always with them both day and night.

He provides the way for His sheep no matter where they may wake up from their lukewarm slumber and discover they are surrounded by "spiritual enemies". God swiftly encircles His blanket of supernatural protection around His own sheep as they maneuver about in the fold.

Thou hast beset me behind and before, and laid thine hand upon me. (Psalms 139:5 KJV)

God follows behind and is in front leading every step we take. He is always ready to steer us down His chosen pathway if we lean upon own our own understanding heading towards the wrong turn at a fork in the road. He is always guiding us, gently nudging us as necessary, as we make our way through this life on our walk towards and eternal home with Him.

And thine ears shall hear a word behind thee, saying, This is the way, walk ye in it, when ye turn to the right hand, and when ye turn to the left. (Isaiah 30:21 KJV)

I have set the LORD always before me: because he is at my right hand, I shall not be moved. (Psalms 16:8 KJV)

On the left hand, where he doth work, but I cannot behold him: he hideth himself on the right hand, that I cannot see him: (Job 23:9 KJV)

God surrounds us completely: He is walking beside us, to the right, and left of our path and He is at our shoulder and hovering above as we walk with Him.

How excellent is thy lovingkindness, O God! therefore the children of men put their trust under the shadow of thy wings. (Ps 36:7 KJV)

God hovers above us and protecting us in the shadows of His wing. He places us underneath His wings protecting us from dark spiritual forces and harm according to His will for our life.

The eternal God is thy refuge, and underneath are the everlasting arms: and he shall thrust out the enemy from before thee; and shall say, Destroy them. (Deuteronomy 33:27 KJV)

God's arms are underneath us, holding us upright as necessary. He lifts His children out of the miry clay, setting them on a firm foundation, setting us down gently with His loving arms.

Know ye not that ye are the temple of God, and that the Spirit of God dwelleth in you? (1 Corinthians 3:16 KJV)

His Spirit lives within the heart of each child of God. It is a refuge in times of spiritual persecution and tribulation. The Lord's strong right arm comes up against the enemies and dark spiritual forces who are working against His children as they sojourn in this world, living sacrificially unto Him.

The Bible tells us clearly the Lord has us completely surrounded by His protecting love on all sides and even above and beneath us. This shows the depth of His great love for us and His care and concern for our spiritual and physical well-being.

FOR FURTHER CONTEMPLATION:

The next time you begin to contemplate and fear about a situation which surrounds you; remember how well the Lord has you covered in His divine care and protection. Look His great love, mercy, and grace instead of your troubling circumstances. Glance at your circumstances and intently Gaze His holiness.

Hagar Ran Away

But Abram said unto Sarai, Behold, thy maid is in thy hand; do to her as it pleaseth thee. And when Sarai dealt hardly with her, she fled from her face. And the angel of the LORD found her by a fountain of water in the wilderness, by the fountain in the way to Shur. And he said, Hagar, Sarai's maid, whence camest thou? and whither wilt thou go? And she said, I flee from the face of my mistress Sarai. And the angel of the LORD said unto her, Return to thy mistress, and submit thyself under her hands." (Genesis 16:6-9 KJV)

Has someone dealt with you hardly? The word hardly in the Greek is *awnaw*. It means to be dealt with harshly, or treated severely. And when Sarai dealt hardly with her, she fled from her face.

Sarai harshly treated Hagar, allowing raw emotion and anger to ensue over Hagar who was carrying her husband Abram's child. It was Sarai's own idea to circumvent God's plan, bringing Abram a child by her own means, even if it meant her husband was to lie with her maid Hagar, Sarai pushed an ungodly union between them to fruition. From then on, Sarai dealt hardly with her, and she soon fled from her face. Hagar ran away from these relational problems staring her in the face. She was looking to find peace and relief by running away from the situation before her.

How often do you want to run away from issues plaguing your closest relationships? A husband not treating his wife with respect, children who have no honor for their parents, brothers or sisters unable to put away the sibling rivalry from their youth. Family relationship issues plague many homes today. Many choose the same route Hagar did, running away from their problems instead of dealing with them.

Hagar had obediently followed through with her earthly master Sarai's scheme to produce an heir for Abram through sinful disobedience. Not only did Sarai come up with this half-baked plan, but she led the other two down the path of this sinful scheme. Each person is responsible for their own wicked choices in God's court of justice. God does not participate in the "blame game" which is played out to epidemic proportions today, nor does he hold to the "kangaroo courts of man's justice.

What problems or situations might you run away from in your life? Is it time to lay down the game token you have been fondly clutching from the "blame game" and picking up the Word of God instead? The Word of God has answers and direction for all issues of life.

God did send an angel to seek out after Hagar that day. The angel did find her in desperation and anguish by a source of water in the wilderness:

And the angel of the LORD found her by a fountain of water in the wilderness, by the fountain in the way to Shur. And he said, Hagar, Sarai's maid, whence camest thou? and whither wilt thou go? And she said, I flee from the face of my mistress Sarai. And the angel of the LORD said unto her, Return to thy mistress, and submit thyself under her hands. And the angel of the LORD said unto her, I will multiply thy seed exceedingly, that it shall not be numbered for multitude. (Genesis 16:7-10 KJV)

The angel of the Lord did appeal to Hagar to return in submission to Sarai her earthly master, promising to number heir of Abram exceedingly. To Hagar on one hand this request from the angel must have seemed outlandish. Why would she want to choose to return to a situation that was laced with rejection and anger? However, on the other hand, this angel of the Lord had been sent by God to come to Hagar as she lay in udder desperation, knowing she was in a situation way over her head. Clearly this promise from God spoken by the Angel of the Lord to multiply her seed was from a merciful and loving God who heard her desperate cries. Just as He hears our desperate cry today, He heard her prayers and pleading.

Call unto me, and I will answer thee, and shew thee great and mighty things, which thou knowest not. (Jeremiah 33:3 KJV)

Hagar did choose to follow the leading of the angel of the Lord. She turned away from her sin, from her rejection, and trusted in God to fulfill His promises to her as she became obedient unto Him.

FOR FURTHER CONTEMPLATION:

Do you hear the Lord calling for you to turn about and be obedient unto Him today? Clutch tightly onto the promises contained in His Word for your life no matter what circumstances you see swirling about you.

But God Moments

And the LORD said unto Moses, Wherefore criest thou unto me? speak unto the children of Israel, that they go forward: But lift thou up thy rod, and stretch out thine hand over the sea, and divide it: and the children of Israel shall go on dry ground through the midst of the sea." (Exodus 14:15-16 KJV)

God provides awesome protection for each of His own spiritual family, just as He provided for the Israelites at the Red Sea to escape certain destruction. In their own human understanding of circumstances surrounding them, to the Israelites there seemed no way out, they were "boxed in" or "stuck in the mud" so to speak at shore of the Red Sea. But God provided a way when there was no logical way for the Israelites to escape.

In the same miraculous manner He provided His divine protection and way forth from the oven for Daniel and his three friends as they faced certain death in the three times at hot fiery furnace. They all escaped certain death in an oven of flames without even a hint of smoke or cinder encroaching upon them. Other examples include Jonah trapped inside the belly of the whale, Paul as he faced many adverse and harrowing situations in New Testament times. Joseph remained unharmed through situations in the Old Testament times under the law, at the hands of his evil and uncaring brothers, who had left him to die in a lowly pit but then offered him for sale to slave traders for money instead. Joseph chose to help his own brothers in their time of great need during a severe famine in later years of their life.

"But God moments" are moments of divine victory in Him for those who are willing to drop all and follow His lead and call on their life; even in times when life just does not seem to make sense in our limited viewpoint from earth.

These great Biblical examples illustrate God can provide just what is needed, when it is needed, along with His divine protection and guidance, even when we have faltering moments of doubt becoming sore afraid, He remains steadfast working in us and through us.

That is why we are to walk by faith in Him and not by sight of circumstances surrounding us:

(For we walk by faith, not by sight:) (2 Corinthians 5:7 KJV)

FOR FURTHER CONTEMPLATION:

Do you allow Him to work in your "But God" moments? Or do you grab the "steering wheel" out of His nail scared hands, steering your own pathway through any adversities which are staring you smack in the face?

Hurdles Can Be Self-Inflicted Barriers

Hurdles to enlarging our faith are often self-created. A barrier, a hindrance, or wall to greater faith encompasses or is attracted to attitudes such as doubt, inadequacy, selfish desires, pride, stubbornness, and fear; all of which can get in the way of the temperature of our faith in God.

These hindrances are deep-rooted spiritual matters of the heart. They are further entwined by our often stubborn will and mindset, in constant enmity against the things of God, entertaining a bent towards the darkened ways of the world. These inner skirmishes and heated times of turmoil often short-circuit our trust, inhibiting us from obeying God's will in our life.

A feeling of inadequacy can likewise hinder us from climbing out onto the edge of the limb where God has called us to stand firm in an exercise of faith. Like Moses, we can quickly conclude our abilities are not up to par for the job the Lord has laid at our feet. We begin hastily stepping backwards, offering excuses rolling off our tongue to God for our lack of faith and trust in Him and His divine abilities. We fail to lift up our eyes from our immediate circumstances, and place our eyes upon the character and greatness of God who has already ascertained the final victory for us as we crawl out on the edge of the limb for His glory and honor.

Past failures, if we let them, can greatly limit our insight and perception of a situation immediately before us. Instead of viewing the situation through the holy lens of God we peer into the situation using glasses manufactured by the world. Satan likes to constantly remind us about our past, parading our faults and failures before us. To end this procession of doom and gloom we must change our focus to view or contemplate upon the glorious things of God and His truth from words of His Scripture.

Gender and race barriers can impede our fruitful exercise of faith such as witnessing the gospel message of hope to others. We can get tangled up in "religious rules and hang-ups" impeding our march forward sowing the seed of the gospel just as the disciples did in the book of John. The disciples, being Jewish, were hindered and indifferent towards the Samaritans, not even dwelling about the immediate environment in their midst, let alone sharing in any conversation or life events together. The attitudes between them were mutual on both sides; racial hatred and disdain.

Christ marched beyond these traditional stumbling blocks and witnessed to the Samaritan woman at the well in the middle of the day, bringing her to her knees, and unto saving faith with Him. Christ's example should move us to seek out and witness to lost souls beyond racial barriers society or man's traditions have tried to firmly erect in the middle of the pathway.

Sin not repented from serves as an insurmountable wall as well for obtaining greater and deeper faith in serving Christ. Sin creates an open and wide ravine between us and our relationship with Christ. This ravine continues to widen and deepen as our sin takes root and grows the problem grows, cutting off or choking our spiritual communication with Christ. This lack of communication causes our faith to diminish, while our ear for the wickedness of the world abounds or grows. When our faith shrinks because of sin we find ourselves outside the "holy circle", like a leper outside the gate in the Old Testament, far away from the center of events and ultimately without possessing the will of God a spiritual U-turn away from a close relationship with Him. Repenting and capitulating from our sins brings us back into a close relationship with Christ and once again inside the know of His "holy circle" spiritually understanding His will for our life as it is revealed unto us. Our faith builds upon the mercy and goodness of Christ according to our close and personal relationship with Him; not of anything we can do for ourselves.

Our priorities can be a barrier to growing deeper in faith. If we choose to serve the things of this world foremost, not acknowledging and obeying His priorities for our life, our relationship gap with Him will widen. Christ will not take a back seat in our life, but demands the driver's seat, guiding us along the narrow path as He sees fit for His glory and honor. If we only allow Him to occupy the backseat He is no longer directing our pathway through the jungle of this world; but we are heading out upon a crooked pathway of our own choosing and direction.

When nagging doubts, walls, and obstructions are allowed to assault our minds on a continual basis they create a lack of faith and spiritual disdain in our life. The good news is these barriers can be overcome and stepped over with diligent study of Scripture and persistent prayer, helping to dislodge uncertainty and building a bridge to a deeper relationship with Christ. God promises His provision in a right relationship with Him.

But thanks be to God, which giveth us the victory through our Lord Jesus Christ. Therefore, my beloved brethren, be ye stedfast, unmoveable, always abounding in the work of the Lord, forasmuch as ye

know that your labour is not in vain in the Lord. (1 Corinthians 15:57-58 KJV)

It is not hard to be a Christian. The bible says the way of the sinner is hard. There is suffering in the world for the saved and the lost. But there is joy in the Lord. There is joy and rest in following His will for our life. All it takes is faith and trust in His promises.

Come unto me, all ye that labour and are heavy laden, and I will give you rest. Take my yoke upon you, and learn of me; for I am meek and lowly in heart: and ye shall find rest unto your souls. For my yoke is easy, and my burden is light. (Matthew 11:28-30 KJV)

Good understanding giveth favour: but the way of transgressors is hard. (Proverbs 13:15 KJV)

FOR FURTHER CONTEMPLATION:

Victory in Christ is a settled issue. His victory for us was finished on the cross 2000 years ago. We have no excuse for any lack of faith in following Christ's will for our life. When He asks you to "Get in the boat...," and allow Him to take command of the helm, do not hesitate, obey His command.

Paul Was Willing to Suffer

(Philippians 3:10 KJV) That I may know him, and the power of his resurrection, and the fellowship of his sufferings, being made conformable unto his death;

The progression of inspiration by God upon Paul's thoughts in this chapter reaches its culmination here. Paul had willingly, not begrudgingly, suffered the loss of all accomplishments and advancement so that he might win Christ and His righteousness. It was that I may know him, and the power of his resurrection, and the fellowship of his sufferings. His desire was to know Christ. Paul had met many worldly men, but he longed to know God. Jesus said in John 17:3, "And this is life eternal, that they might know thee the only true God, and Jesus Christ, whom thou hast sent."

It is one thing to receive Christ. It is quite another thing to get to know Him altogether or in an intimately personal spiritual fashion. That was Paul's desire. The word "know" refers to knowledge grounded on personal experience. That is, to know by experience. Paul desired to develop an understanding and knowledge of Christ by personal bond with Him.

Moreover, he also longed to know "the power of his resurrection." He likely refers generally to the power of God which raised Jesus from the dead. This is the very same power God uses to resurrect sinners from the grip of death while in our natural sin nature. Paul longed to have the supernatural power of God abounding in his life and ministry to overflowing capacity.

Finally, he longed to know "the fellowship of his sufferings." Even as Christ had suffered on our behalf, Paul looked forward to sharing in those sufferings. He had by this point in life gone through considerable persecution. He knew what it meant. But he joyed in it knowing, in some small measure, he was participating in sufferings like His Savior did. The majority of Christians today know little or nothing of what it means to suffer for Christ. Paul did and he longed to so experience that suffering to share in that which Christ suffered for us.

Paul knew he could very well face the executioner at Rome. Thus, he was willing to be made conformable unto his death. Though he hoped to be delivered therefrom, if it came to that, he was more than willing to be conformed to what happened to His Lord—death by execution. For him to live was Christ, but to die was gain.

FOR FURTHER CONTEMPLATION:

Do you seek to gain spiritually in Christ including loss of worldly treasure as God deems necessary while sojourning upon this earth?

The Twenty Four Hour Media Circus

Our physical bodies require a steady and balanced diet of nutrition; our souls and spiritual fortitude or good health require a steady diet of scripture and contemplation upon God's Word.

Don't allow the world to feed you heaping portions of calamities and bad news. Instead feast upon the riches of Christ. Empty out the trash pile containing world's wickedness in your mind and fill up on delectable helpings of His Word, renewing you mindset and heart attitude towards the peaceful and orderly things of God.

I beseech you therefore, brethren, by the mercies of God, that ye present your bodies a living sacrifice, holy, acceptable unto God, which is your reasonable service. And be not conformed to this world: but be ye transformed by the renewing of your mind, that ye may prove what is that good, and acceptable, and perfect, will of God. (Romans 12:1-2 KJV)

The "twenty four hour news buffet" is based upon feeding sensationalism to drama hungry viewers. This hyped up diet of bad news is rehashed over and over again leading many individuals to worry, fret, and fear needlessly. Prominent stories are featured which are based upon catastrophes and sensational events. The main idea is to keep the audience's attention, capitalizing on a diet of dire happenings, keeping audiences enthralled, even at the expense of another's great pain and suffering. Good ratings make big dollars and therefore make big news. It is a big media circle, or media circus which thrives on making big drama and bucks.

Sometimes even stories and events not ordinarily intense make the news cycle as the producers artificially amp up the drama to a new level, catching the attention of a host of viewers. This makes more common situations seem more intense, more palatable to the "news buffet mindset" than the actual story is in real life.

Hopelessness and horror sells prime time airtime. There is always some cliff one is about to fall over, under, on, or off. Subconsciously this hopelessness causes the willing viewing audience to feel hopeless and look to the future with a dismal and bleak outlook; discounting the many promises of God.

 It is not couth to the world's "entertainment mindset" to look towards God, inward, upward and outward with hope, faith, and love as the Bible directs us to live our lives. This is living vertically towards Christ, not horizontal looking towards man's views and opinions to satisfy man's innate desire for the peace of God.

The media and news circus has even gone down the path of dishing the blame towards God subliminally. No wonder there is discontent and grumbling even among professing Christians living in this world. Many try to live on the fence, between right and wrong, with their foot dangling down in this wretched world. The twenty four hour news cycle operates most often in enmity against the things of God. Many Christians continue to feed from the trough of this sensational news buffet, often many are more up to date on the latest news than they are with understanding their Bible; unable to rightly divide God's Word. This is a sad, but true, fact.

I am not proposing to completely ignore the news. A small dose of news to stay informed and a large portion of Bible daily help fuel a vibrant, spiritually healthy approach to keeping up with what is happening in world. Having a heart right with God first and foremost before viewing news events maintains an understanding and purpose according to His will and way; keeping our minds spiritually healthy and at rest while surrounded by His perfect peace.

I am crucified with Christ: nevertheless I live; yet not I, but Christ liveth in me: and the life which I now live in the flesh I live by the faith of the Son of God, who loved me, and gave himself for me. (Galatians 2:20 KJV)

FOR FURTHER CONTEMPLATION:

Watch the news with the heart and mind of God and cling to His promises as you live in the world in His strength.

Self-Sacrifice in Serving Him

Self-sacrifice is the way of life in a personal relationship of victory in Jesus Christ. We must die daily to Him, hourly, or even minute by the minute, if necessary, keeping our relationship right with Him. Each time we choose to obey his commandments we sacrifice our natural inclinations and desires for things of the world. This personal sacrifice is tied directly into the pattern of burnt offerings taught in the Old Testament book of Leviticus. The book of Leviticus was written to provide details about truly worshiping Him in Old Testament times and for today as we live and exist in the end times.

The Burnt Offering is ultimately a picture of Jesus sacrificing all, even unto His death on the cross for us. This provides a picture of how we are to sacrificially live for Him today. This offering was originally accomplished through the burning of animal sacrifices in Old Testament times but was not efficient for removal of sin, only covering it.

We must choose to lay aside our life sacrificially to partake of a holy relationship with Him. A sacrificial life is all about laying down our life and picking up our cross and honoring and giving glory to Him; nothing to do about us.

Not only are we called to lay aside any and all sin that might beset us, hindering our relationship with Him, but sacrificially laying our sin at His feet so He can reduce this heap to nothing but ash; just as the Old Testament sacrifices were reduced to ash. He reduced our sin debt to nothing, or marked "paid in full" by His precious shed blood sacrifice for all mankind upon the cross; reducing our sin debt to a zero balance on our personal ledger.

We are to consider anything that hinders our relationship with Him to be worthy of this burning process and offer those sweet-smelling sacrifices up to Him. This sacrificial process goes against our natural bent towards self-gratification and the "all about me" worldly viewpoint of life. What is in it for me, about me, and how I can gain the most from this situation at hand is the perspective we often encounter from those living in this world. This viewpoint has nothing to do with Jesus Christ or the great sacrifice He made for us. Living for self is in direct opposition or in enmity of living for Jesus Christ.

But what things were gain to me, those I counted loss for Christ. Yea doubtless, and I count all things but loss for the excellency of the knowledge of Christ Jesus my Lord: for whom I have suffered the loss of all things, and do count them but dung, that I may win Christ, And be found in him, not having mine own righteousness, which is of the law, but that which is through the faith of Christ, the righteousness which is of God by faith: (Philippians 3:7-9KJV)

FOR FURTHER CONTEMPLATION:

What is He asking you sacrifice in order to gain a deeper relationship with Him? He promises to pull us forth and stand us upright in positional standing before Him, despite trials, sufferings, and sacrifices. Allowing us to come forth as gold if we allow Him to try us and test our faith in Him through the fires of life.

But he knoweth the way that I take: when he hath tried me, I shall come forth as gold. (Job 10:23) KJV

God's Gardens

And the LORD God planted a garden eastward in Eden; and there he put the man whom he had formed. (Genesis 2:8 KJV)

The first garden was The Garden of Eden. It was a place of splendid beauty, perfection a lush tropical paradise. It is where the tree of life was planted. The weather is always perfect and the growing conditions are primed for further lush development. It was not hard for man to feel at peace when surrounded by such elegant and vibrantly colored flowers and fauna. Our Lord is a master gardener. This Garden of Eden was created in the beginning by God giving honor and glory to Him, and secondly for an atmosphere for man, giving him a place to live, providing protection and provision for his food. This garden was flawless until sin entered into the environment through man and his freewill. When sin entered the picture instead of living thriving plant life; death entered this picture perfect garden filled with life.

Not only did God create this lush environment of the Garden of Eden but He also had a hand in creating the Garden of Gethsemane . This garden was where Jesus found a place of rest, peace, and most importantly time alone with His Father in prayer. This was the garden where His disciples found rest, even falling asleep, instead of remaining steadfast in prayer:

And when he rose up from prayer, and was come to his disciples, he found them sleeping for sorrow, And said unto them, Why sleep ye? rise and pray, lest ye enter into temptation. (Luke 22:45-46 KJV)

The Garden of Gethsemane was where Jesus faced His greatest agony, knowing the will of His Father and accepting it, surrendering to it in perfect obedience to His Father's will.

The third garden is the garden of Golgotha, or commonly called the place of the skull. This is the garden where Jesus was buried. This garden was near the crucifixion site but banished outside the gates of the city. It was not a family burial site for Jesus, but one given by a friend Joseph of Arimathaea, for burying Him since a tomb was needed in haste to bring His body down before the Sabbath, as was the custom in those days. Jesus did not have a place to lay His head while alive or in death; as all His treasures were laid up in Heaven with His Father and not a part of this earth.

In Revelation chapter 22 the final garden is mentioned:

In the midst of the street of it, and on either side of the river, was there the tree of life, which bare twelve manner of fruits, and yielded her fruit every month: and the leaves of the tree were for the healing of the nations. (Revelation 22:2 KJV)

Notice this garden is inside the city, not banished outside as a dirty and unclean place; not relevant to be included inside the city gates. This garden is pure and holy. Secondly the tree of life from the Garden of Eden resides in this atmosphere of a perfect garden with refreshing water of life flowing around it. This last garden is in the new heaven and new earth. It once again provides provision and protection for man and most importantly his spiritual restoration.

This last garden wholly restores man's spiritual fellowship with our Lord and Creator God. This garden removes all hint of sin prior to man entering within and replacing sin it with the whole perfection of God so that any who reside within are without any sin whatsoever and perfect as He is perfect.

FOR FURTHER CONTEMPLATION:

Christ is the Master Gardener. There is no garden here on earth to compare to any of His gardens; especially the last and perfect garden in the new heaven and earth yet to be revealed.

Bringing Every Thought Into Captivity

(For the weapons of our warfare are not carnal, but mighty through God to the pulling down of strong holds;) Casting down imaginations, and every high thing that exalteth itself against the knowledge of God, and bringing into captivity every thought to the obedience of Christ; (2 Corinthians 10:4-5 KJV)

Bring into captivity to Christ every thought to the obedience of Christ. Wow, what a huge task this is in today's world as we get assaulted from every side with facts, figures, information, and much disinformation. Minds are being compromised from all angles at lightning speed. Satan and his minions are busy spinning to and fro spewing out wicked and dark spiritual assaulting material via television, radio, internet, any voice medium they can facilitate for their wicked leaning dark endeavors.

Spiritual warfare is a monumental and spiritually and mentally challenging for many Christians. Facing battles is most often an uphill climb for those who profess the name of Jesus. At the first sign or indication of a spiritual skirmish; many well-meaning but weak Christians choose to hastily lay down their sword as the spiritual mêlée begins to gear up around them and run off in the opposite direction. This attitude is akin to lying down like a spiritual doormat; allowing those who oppose God's Word run ram shod over them with fiery darts. Any areas of skin left open and exposed or containing a chink in their spiritual armor, as described in Ephesians chapter six, are assaulted, battered, and maimed by the devil's dark spiritual bullets straight from a crossbow of the god of this earth's army unto their exposed flesh.

Many face huge spiritual dilemmas simply and foremost because they are living weakened and biblically illiterate lives; never having placed scriptures inside their heart nor any spiritual armor about themselves outwardly as well as having the Holy Spirit dwelling inside for the utmost of spiritual protection. God desires His own family attire or cloak themselves tightly in His supernatural protection; but will never forcedly place His armor upon anyone.

Is YOUR mind and heart filled to overflowing with scripture for exposing the lies and twisted beliefs of satan as you face spiritual battles in His strength and power on a daily basis? Do you have the ammunition, or "spiritual bullets" God provides for these battles ready at hand, to expose and destroy spiritually poisoned darts satan and his minions hurl violently towards anyone who boldly proclaim the name Jesus upon the doorway of their soul.

Read Ephesians 6: 10-18 and contemplate further facing spiritual battles in God's armor and strength. This is the narrow pathway leading to spiritual victory in our thoughts and actions while we sojourn upon this earth.

FOR FURTHER CONTEMPLATION:

Look to Him, listen to Him, focus intently upon His Word, and be blanketed in His supernatural protection; both inwardly and outwardly, as you walk on the narrow path through this life towards heaven.

Remember Lot's Wife?

Are you walking daily with Christ but continuing to peer back over your shoulder at the past? Embarking on a personal relationship with Christ and walking daily with Him does not mix with living in the flesh in a sinful lifestyle. The fleshly lifestyle always ends in physical and spiritual death.

Remember Lot's wife? She dared to look back, even staring intently over her shoulder even dragging her heels in the sand. She was looking back at the city of Sodom as her family, with aid of an angel was fleeing the utter wickedness in the city. They were running purposely towards freedom and safety with God in the midst of fire and brimstone as they escaped God's righteous anger and fiery judgment.

The Bible states:

But his wife looked back from behind him, and she became a pillar of salt. (Genesis 19:26 KJV)

Whatever utter wickedness a person has forsaken to walk with Christ; whatever web they are caught up in alcohol, drugs, physical abuse, unnatural relations, cheating on a spouse ... if one chooses to live "on the edge of Christianity," dwelling on their past sin by looking over their shoulder they soon begin to stumble, taking baby steps or backward steps in their spiritual relationship with Christ. This leads to "carnal Christianity or worse yet; a wide road to Hell for those who falsely professed Christ from their lips but not sincerely from their heart.

Even Lot, who did escape Sodom with his daughters, eventually pitched his tent towards his past in Sodom:

Then Lot chose him all the plain of Jordan; and Lot journeyed east: and they separated themselves the one from the other. Abram dwelled in the land of Canaan, and Lot dwelled in the cities of the plain, and pitched his tent toward Sodom. (Genesis 13:11-12 KJV)

After his last minute escape from the fire and brimstone of Sodom he lived abundantly in Canaan for a time.

Then He journeyed east, separating himself from Abram. Lot then pitched his tent to face Sodom. This was not a wise choice to make and eventually he found himself once again planted squarely in the middle of the city which was brimming with sin.

The same thing happens often today. We make choices which lead our focus away from Christ and being flocked or surrounded by good spiritual influence of our Christian friends and we begin to focus intently onto the pleasures of this world and allow our view of Christ to dim into the background.

Lot chose to look back on his past which was a seductively sinful lifestyle choosing to turn his back towards the things of Christ. A person does not often fall head first into a vat of sin but rather gradually finds himself edging closer and closer to sin calling our name and drawing in our wicked sinful human nature which is naturally deprived and at home in wickedness.

Before the entering into a danger zone filled with sin and rebellion towards God pick up your tent and turn it towards Christ, surround yourself with spiritually filled friends, and keep that communion with Christ brimming over and over with love, joy, peace, and the promise of eternal life playing in your mind.

FOR FURTHER CONTEMPLATION:

Are you edging closer and closer to a playground full of sin and wickedness? Or are you in the garden with God?

Flesh of Ishmael, the Promise of Isaac

And Abram said, Behold, to me thou hast given no seed: and, lo, one born in my house is mine heir. And, behold, the word of the LORD came unto him, saying, This shall not be thine heir; but he that shall come forth out of thine own bowels shall be thine heir. And he brought him forth abroad, and said, Look now toward heaven, and tell the stars, if thou be able to number them: and he said unto him, So shall thy seed be. (Genesis 15:3-5 KJV)

Abraham was elderly, in his eighties and still yearning for a son, for an heir to carry on His name sake. Sara was still barren these many years and Abraham had not yet received the son God had promised him to provide. The only child to have grown up in their household was eliezer, who was born to a servant, not of Abraham's own loins.

Both he and Sara became impatient, living by sight, losing all faith in the promise of God ever being fulfilled in their lifetime. Sara came up with a plan of her own to provide a son to Abraham, knowing he was desperately seeking a child and she being physically unable to fulfill his desire. Abraham listened intently to Sarah's scheme willingly agreeing to have a son with her maid Hagar.

Abraham allowed his wife to be the leader of his house; having no problem conforming to her leadership and Sara had no problem entering into the role. She was sure God's promise was doomed for failure; and left without hope Sara decided God needed her help in bringing the promise to fruition.

How many times have you eagerly tried stepping into the shoes of God or to sit upon His throne, masterfully orchestrating, maneuvering, and manipulating events or situations because God was unable to deliver the outcome you desired or expected. The outcome which lined up with your own "professional" assessment and timing of the situation? If we are honest, all of us would have to admit we have eagerly pushed God off His throne to readily assume His role of authority in our lives too many times to count over the years.

The promise God made to Abraham concerning Isaac definitely was going to be brought to pass, God never lies always fulfilling any promise, or covenant, He makes but in His timing and way. That is where we fail, to wait upon God in His perfect timing and to trust upon His promises even when we cannot see the end of the situation from our limited viewpoint upon this earth.

Delight thyself also in the LORD; and he shall give thee the desires of thine heart. Commit thy way unto the LORD; trust also in him; and he shall bring it to pass. (Psalms 37:4-5 KJV)

Failure to trust upon God waiting patiently for His holy timing in any given situation is sin. It is a choice mankind makes saying to God, "I can handle this situation much better and quicker than you can or ever will for me."

Some four thousand years later our world is still dealing with the consequences of Abraham's impatient decision to set aside leadership of his own house and blindly follow Sara's convoluted plot for Abraham to lie with her maid Hagar bearing a son as an heir.

God's plan was altogether different. It was an undeniable miracle for Sara in her elder years, to become with child by Abraham providing Isaac as the God designated heir for Abraham's seed. God did provide this miracle heir, just as He promised; bringing to fruition Sara bearing Isaac for Abraham. This promise from God was fulfilled after Abraham willingly followed through with Sara's sinful and rebellious plan as they both gave up on God.

The determined choice both Abraham and Sara made forever changed the landscape and border of Jerusalem. The descendants of Isaac, the promise of God, and the descendants of Ishmael, the work of flesh, continually struggle for control of the land of Israel.

And yes, in our own lives our natural bent for our fleshly desires do struggle against our inner spiritual nature or positional standing in the will of God for our life. Just like Abraham and Sara struggled in ancient biblical times and Paul's spiritual battles with the flesh in the New Testament.

Paul acknowledged having ever-present spiritual battles in His life:

For I know that in me (that is, in my flesh,) dwelleth no good thing: for to will is present with me; but how to perform that which is good I find not. For the good that I would I do not: but the evil which I would not, that I do. Now if I do that I would not, it is no more I that do it, but sin that dwelleth in me. I find then a law, that, when I would do good, evil is present with me. For I delight in the law of God after the inward man: But I see another law in my members, warring against the law of my mind, and bringing me into captivity to the law of sin which is in my members. (Romans 7:18-23 KJV)

It is a process of sanctification throughout our spiritual life as we learn to hand everything over to God and to live a crucified life unto Him; not desiring to dwell or continually inhabit in our fleshly desires in enmity against the things of God.

Abraham, Sara, and Paul, and many other biblical characters, are given to us as examples of failing to wait on God, failing to trust in God, failing to live crucified unto God and the wages of our choice to sin.

The birth of Ishmael will continue to wage spiritual and physical warfare upon this earth until Jesus comes back to wave the final banner of victory coming from the clouds to convey His own spiritual family mmup to heaven unto the throne of God for all who chose to place personal their faith in Him.

FOR FURTHER CONTEMPLATION:

Confessed and unconfessed sin before God both can wage major consequences lasting a lifetime. Sin is grim and must be taken seriously. God paid the price for sin but we still face natural consequences of our sin.

www.ingramcontent.com/pod-product-compliance
Lightning Source LLC
Chambersburg PA
CBHW071458040426
42444CB00008B/1393